Between Hashemites and Zionists

Between Hashemites and Zionists

The Struggle for Palestine 1908–1988

Martin Sicker

HM HOLMES & MEIER New York / London

Published in the United States of America 1989 by
    Holmes & Meier Publishers, Inc.
    30 Irving Place
    New York, N.Y. 10003

Copyright © 1989 by Holmes & Meier Publishers, Inc.
All rights reserved. No part of this book may be reproduced or transmitted in any form or by any electronic or mechanical means now known or to be invented, including photocopying, recording, and information storage and retrieval systems, without permission in writing from the publishers, except by a reviewer who may quote brief passages in a review.

Book design by Dale Cotton

The paper used in this publication meets the requirements of the American National Standard for Permanence of Paper for printed Library Materials, Z39.48-1984.

Library of Congress Cataloging-in-Publication Data

Sicker, Martin.
    Between Hashemites and Zionists.

    Bibliography: p.
    Includes index.
    1. Jewish-Arab relations. 2. Hashimites. 3. Jordan
—Foreign relations. I. Title.
DS119.7.S38195   1989   956   88-32834
ISBN 0-8419-1176-2 (alk. paper)
ISBN 0-8419-1264-5 (pbk. : alk. paper)

Manufactured in the United States of America

For Avi and Adam

Contents

Preface	ix
1 The Anglo-Hashemite Conspiracy	1
2 The Anglo-Zionist Conspiracy	27
3 The Period of Hashemite-Zionist Cooperation	51
4 The Emergence of Hashemite Transjordan	75
5 From Transjordan to Jordan and Back	103
6 Hussein, the Palestinians and Israel	125
Afterword	147
Notes	157
Bibliography	165
Index	171

Preface

Any new book dealing with some aspect of the Arab-Israeli conflict requires an explanation as to why the author believes it was worth writing and why anyone should bother to read it. Writings about the subject abound and it is difficult to imagine what one might have to say about it that has not already been put on paper somewhere. Yet the fact remains that, notwithstanding the enormous literature on the subject published over the last forty years, there is scarcely an issue of international significance that is as poorly understood, by both laymen and statesmen alike, as the Arab-Israeli conflict. It is an issue that seems to preclude dispassionate objectivity. Why this is so should be a question of some considerable interest. It is not, however, the immediate concern of this book.

The burden of this brief work is to attempt to cut through much of the polemical fog that has beset key aspects of the Arab-Israeli issue by recalling the essential background of the problem in its real rather than imaginary political context. For it is only by understanding the real issues behind the Arab-Israeli conflict that there can be any hope of ever finding a way of resolving it, rather than merely papering it over with pious and well-intentioned but largely irrelevant and impracticable solutions.

Preface

As a first step toward such understanding, it is essential to discard the overly simplistic discussions of the problem that begin by postulating its "root cause," a phrase that has become a favorite of contemporary intellectual dilettantes. There are many factors that have contributed to the creation of the Arab-Israeli conflict, but there is no such thing as a "root cause."

Second, it is important to shed one's tendency to be patronizing to the regional parties to the conflict, particularly the Arabs, if one is to grasp the true character of the issues. What this means in practical terms is that leaders must be held accountable for what they do and say, and not treated as minor children whose indiscretions are excused on account of their presumed political immaturity.

Third, it is necessary to understand the Arab-Israeli conflict within the context of its geopolitical realities and not merely in ideological and utopian terms.

Finally, and perhaps most essential of all, we must disabuse ourselves of the tendency to oversimplify for the purpose of analysis and then construe that oversimplification as historical fact.

While this book, as reflected in its title, is about Palestine, it is not primarily about what has become known in recent years as the Palestinian problem, that is, the unfulfilled nationalist aspirations of the Palestinian Arabs, whether or not represented by the Palestine Liberation Organization. Admittedly, the Arabs of Palestine have been the primary victims of the Arab-Israeli conflict. However, it is the Arab states which must bear the major onus for this. As will be seen, the Arab leaders, and most especially the Hashemites, never seriously contemplated the emergence of an Arab Palestinian state and, in fact, took direct steps to preclude one from being created. The fact that the Arabs now favor the establishment of a Palestinian state does not mitigate the fact that by their own self-serving intransigence on this issue forty years ago, when the possibility was imminent and real, that possibility may have been lost entirely, or at the least, for the foreseeable future. The Palestinian Arabs may persist in their struggle for an independent state, but there is no law of history which says that they will or must achieve their goal. One need but recall, to speak only of the Middle East, that both the Kurds and the Armenians

Preface

have actively struggled for an independent homeland for a longer period than the Palestinians, without any prospect of success in the foreseeable future.

The primary concern of this work is to examine the more than seventy-year-long struggle of the Hashemites and the Zionists for the control of Palestine, that is, the area of the earlier British mandate that included the territories of both Cis-Jordan and Trans-Jordan, today occupied by the states of Israel and Jordan. The future of the Palestinian Arabs on both sides of the Jordan River will most likely be determined more by the eventual outcome of this struggle than by the much touted but largely ineffective, if not irrelevant, PLO struggle for the liberation of the country. It is the view of the author that the struggle described in these pages must be clearly understood before one can fully appreciate the role of Jordan in the Arab-Israeli conflict and its ultimate resolution.

The Hashemite-Zionist struggle for Palestine originated with the outbreak of World War I, and has continued in one form or another ever since. It would help to further cloud rather than clarify the character of *this* struggle to describe it as one between Jewish and Arab nationalism. As will be demonstrated, while the Hashemites cloaked themselves in the flag of Arab nationalism for strategical and tactical purposes, their primary interests were far more dynastic than nationalist.

Emerging in an age of rampant nationalism, the spokesmen of modern Zionism saw themselves in an unprecedented historic struggle for the highest of stakes, and were prepared to do whatever they thought necessary to advance their aims. They were well aware of and concerned about the indigenous Arab opposition (which was by no means universal) to their aspirations, but did not see it as an insurmountable barrier. Their goals, as contrasted with those of their antagonists, were geopolitically informed and clearly defined. It will be shown that contemporary lamentations by both Arabs and some Israelis concerning Israel's alleged expansionist aims and tendencies miss the mark completely, and reflect a serious misreading of Zionist history.

The major catalyst of the Hashemite-Zionist struggle was Great Britain, which, for purposes of its own and quite unintentionally, helped precipitate, aggravate and perpetuate the conflict, with-

Preface

out contributing very much toward a viable solution during its period of tenure as the dominant power in the region. British policy makers, acting sometimes as shrewd imperial strategists, sometimes as blatant opportunists, and frequently as proverbial bulls in a china shop, will be shown to bear a heavy responsibility for the tragic history of modern Palestine. It will be seen that British policy was basically neither pro-Zionist nor pro-Arab; it was designed exclusively to serve British interests, which often conflicted with those of both Jews and Arabs.

The world in which the Hashemite-Zionist struggle emerged was one of realpolitik, and it is in such a world that the struggle continues to this day, with the United States replacing Britain as the major external power upon which both protagonists are critically dependent in a variety of ways for their well-being.

The future of Israeli-Jordanian relations, including the viability or even desirability of the much proclaimed "Jordan Option" as the solution of the increasingly volatile West Bank problem, cannot be assessed realistically without an unabashed look at its rather checkered past. It is the purpose of this book to provide such a review of the past as the basis for a clear-eyed view of the future.

Between Hashemites and Zionists

1

The Anglo-Hashemite Conspiracy

The house of the Beni Hashem was descended in the male line from the Prophet's daughter Fatima. The Hashemites, by their lineage, were thus the most prominent clan of the Koreish, in whose tribal lands the holy cities of Mecca and Medina were to be found. By tradition, a Hashemite was always chosen as the titular ruler of the area, the sherif or emir of Mecca, and protector of the holy places. This made them, by definition, the most important extended family in all of Islam. By an astute use of their prominence, coupled with a sure knowledge of Bedouin tribal politics, the Hashemites had also long succeeded in achieving an ascendancy among the indigenous people of the northern Arabian district of the Hejaz. At the turn of the twentieth century, Hejaz was a vilayet of the Ottoman Empire, and was ruled by a Turkish governor in Mecca supported by a garrison of some seven thousand troops. The holy cities, however, were exempt from taxation and conscription for military service and were in practice administered by the sherif.

It had been a long-standing Ottoman practice to help assure control of the sultan's far-flung possessions by holding members of the prominent families of those lands hostage in Constantinople. Thus, for fifteen years, Hussein ibn Ali, the thirty-seventh in the line of descent from the Prophet, had been detained with his wife and sons in the Ottoman capital. During that period, Hussein became a well-known figure in Constantinople and had even been appointed a member of the Council of State.

For Hussein and the Hashemites, 1908 turned out to be a most propitious year. Three events took place that year that were to have far-reaching implications for the future of the Middle East. First, there was a revolution in Turkey which brought the relatively progressive "Young Turks" into power. Even though the Sultan, Abdul-Hamid II, was allowed to keep his throne, the empire was now ruled by the Committee of Union and Progress. Second, the Hejaz Railway, begun by Abdul-Hamid in 1900 to provide a link with the holy places of Islam in Arabia, reached Medina. While its ostensible purpose was to facilitate the pilgrimages of large numbers of Muslims coming from around the world, the Turks did not build the railroad exclusively out of religious motivations. It was also intended to provide a vehicle for the rapid deployment of troops to the distant provinces of Arabia, which were always seething with instability and the threat of rebellion. It turned out, however, that the railroad served to exacerbate the problem rather than provide a means for its containment. Much of the tribal economy of the Hejaz, and a major source of the sherif's revenues, was derived and frequently extorted from the important caravan trade that passed through the territory en route to the holy cities. The coming of the railroad effectively destroyed the caravan trade, having a devastating impact on the tribal economy. This, in turn, tended to increase rather than decrease the volatility of the Hejaz. Finally, the position of grand sherif of Mecca became vacant. The incumbent, whose opposition to Turkish designs made him no longer acceptable to the Sublime Porte (Ottoman government), had been deposed by the Turks, while their choice as his successor died unexpectedly of an apoplectic stroke.

The vacancy in the sherifate presented Hussein with an unprecedented opportunity. He decided to nominate himself for the important position. He wrote to the sultan: "Whereas through the death of my uncle Sherif Abdulillah ibn Mohammed, Emir of Mecca, which followed the deposition of my cousin Sherif Ali Abdullah ibn Mohammed, the Emirate has been rendered vacant; and whereas I am the oldest of the Hashemite family and have first claim to the office of my forefathers, I beg to request His Majesty the Sultan graciously to grant me my rights, which are as well known to him as are my friendship and loyalty."[1] Hussein's application received a mixed reception at the Porte. There appears to have been some difference of opinion regarding his political suitability for the post, one of the most prominent in the Muslim world next to the sultan himself, who was also the caliph, or spiritual head of Islam. Abdul-Hamid was distrustful of Hussein and was therefore disinclined to appoint him to such a sensitive position. The Young Turks, on the other hand, for reasons that are unclear, since Hussein was certainly not a progressive who might be attractive to them, supported his candidacy. Perhaps they did so more out of spite for the sultan than out of a wish to see Hussein in Mecca. In any case, within a matter of days, Hussein received a medal from the sultan for his services to the Porte along with his appointment as the grand sherif of Mecca. Hussein and his family returned to the Hejaz early in December 1908.

The significance and status of the emir of the Hejaz and sherif of Mecca had clearly declined in importance over the previous decades. Some of the traditional privileges of the sherif had been discontinued. In effect he had become a figurehead without much real power. The latter was exercised by the Turkish *vali*, or governor. Hussein moved aggressively to restore the power and prestige of his office. He quickly reestablished Hashemite hegemony over the tribal confederations of the Hejaz. He asserted the ascendancy of sherifian authority over that of the *vali* and increasingly challenged the instructions coming from the Porte through failure to comply and procrastination. According to the acting British consul in Jeddah, by 1914 the sherif was "the sole monarch of the Hedjaz and his word was law in this country. The Grand Shereef is naturally opposed to any reform and wants that everything should run in ancient rut. All departments in Mecca and Jeddah were under the authoritative guidance of the Shereef and the Turkish Government was only in name. Every Vali who came here during the last five years had to be either slave of the Grand Shereef or be summarily dismissed."[2]

Particularly irksome to the Porte was Hussein's refusal to allow continued construction of the Hejaz Railway from Medina south to Mecca. It was not in his interest to make it easier for the Turks to send troops to Mecca. He also undertook, on his own initiative, some inconclusive attempts to bring some of the tribes to the east of the Hejaz under his suzerainty. These steps earned him the enmity of the Committee of Union and Progress, which responded to his challenge to their authority by attempting to radically revise the traditional status of the Hejaz. They insisted that it henceforth be treated as any other vilayet in the empire, fully subject to taxation and conscription. As a practical matter, such a revision in status would have abolished the emirate. Hussein fought back for his political survival with the only means at his disposal. He agitated against the Turks among the people of the holy cities who would be most affected by the Turkish actions. He was soon able to threaten Constantinople with a full-scale insurrection in the very heart of Islam. Recognizing the impact such an occurrence might have on the rest of the empire, the Turks backed down. Hussein's relatively easy and bloodless victory whetted his appetite for further challenges to Turkish rule.

Having transformed the sherifate into a potent factor in the politics of the region, Hussein and the Hashemites achieved new stature in Constantinople. His second eldest son, Abdullah, now returned there to serve in the Turkish parliament as the deputy for Mecca, and had even been offered the position of governor-general of Yemen. Nonetheless, Hussein's challenge to Constantinople's authority was not forgiven. He understood only too well, after long exposure to the Byzantine politics of the capital, that the Young Turks would exploit any opportunity they might find to weaken and ultimately depose him. In reaction, Hussein began to seek allies among other disaffected Arab leaders with whom he might make common cause against the Turks when necessary. He began to establish surreptitious contacts with the fledgling Arab nationalist societies in Syria that had been driven underground by Turkish persecution. As observed by James Morris, "Almost from the moment he became Grand Sherif, Hussein was active, sometimes blatantly, sometimes discreetly, sometimes selfishly, sometimes purely fortuitously, in the movement for Arab sovereignty."[3] Hussein was on a virtually irreversible collision course with the Turkish regime, and was prepared to exploit any significant opportunity to enhance and consolidate his position that was presented to him. Fortuitously, the clouds of war that were gathering over Europe early in 1914 created some unique opportunities for the sherif to pursue his ambitions on a broader scale than he had ever imagined.

For decades, the imperial position in the Indian subcontinent was Great Britain's primary concern beyond Europe. To protect its interests there, the British had long engaged in the "Great Game" to block Russian imperial expansion into Afghanistan and Chinese Turkestan. They had gone to war to prevent the collapse of Turkey in the mid-nineteenth century in order to sustain the existing regional balance of power, and had been the traditional ally of the sultans against the tsars. It was thus with great concern that they now witnessed the emergence of a Turco-German relationship that seemed likely to result in an alliance against Britain in the war that loomed on the horizon. Of particular concern to Britain was the plain geographical fact that the Suez Canal was located practically alongside the edge of the Turkish frontier. The canal was the key to effective British access to its Asian empire, and its security was a matter of the highest priority. Its proximity to Turkey posed an unacceptable potential threat. To further compound the problem of a Turco-German alliance was the fact of the earlier completion of the Berlin-to-Baghdad Railway, which passed through Turkish territory. German access through Turkey to the Persian Gulf could pose a possible threat to the sea lines of communication to the east. And then there was also the matter of the Hejaz Railway.

Although the Hejaz Railway did have some military significance in that it could be used to bring reinforcements into the Arabian peninsula, it was not that aspect of it that was of primary concern to Whitehall. The British were far more interested in and worried about its religious significance. The Hejaz Railway, notwithstanding the opposition on the part of the Bedouin of the Hejaz to it because of economic reasons, and on the part of the sherif because of its significance for his freedom of action in Mecca, was extraordinarily popular throughout the Muslim world, including India, for the most prosaic of reasons. It reduced the physical burden of the pilgrimage to Mecca from an exhausting six-week trip on a camel to a five-day, relatively comfortable train ride. The sultan, who had built the line that had already reached as far as Medina, was also the caliph of Islam and was actively engaged in attempting, through a variety of means, to promote pan-Islamic sentiment as a way of buttressing the ties that were barely holding the Ottoman Empire together. This presented the British with a dilemma of the first order. Ruling over more than seventy million Muslims in India and another sixteen million in the Nile basin, Britain was responsible for the world's greatest Muslim population. There was thus a reasonable fear that a promotion of Muslim unrest, particularly by the Turkish sultan-caliph, could be used to wreak havoc with British imperial interests in Africa and Asia.

The British were highly vulnerable in this regard. They knew it, and so did their enemy. Once Britain openly declared itself against a Germany in alliance with Muslim Turkey, it was widely expected that the British Empire in the East would soon undergo convulsions leading to its dissolution. This perception was clearly reflected in a letter from the chief of the imperial German general staff, Count von Moltke, to his foreign ministry. Moltke declared that the initiation of "insurrection in India, Egypt and the Caucasus . . . is of utmost importance. Thanks to the Pact with Turkey, the Foreign Ministry will be able to realize these ideas and to arouse the fanaticism of Islam."[4] Part of the German plan as outlined by the foreign ministry was to turn Anglo-Egyptian army units against the British by advising them that the sultan-caliph would soon declare war on England. The missions assigned to the Egyptian troops were to wipe out the British officer corps, make the Suez Canal inoperative, and sabotage communications, railways and port installations in Port Said, Suez and Alexandria. The signal that would trigger the actions by the Egyptian troops was to be a frontal attack on the canal by twenty to thirty thousand Turkish troops supported by some seventy thousand Bedouins under Hussein, sherif of Mecca, whose cooperation in this assault on the British in Egypt was expected.

Hussein, however, quickly recognized the relatively significant role that the Hejaz could play in a British-Turkish conflict in the Middle East. A large Bedouin force could effectively harass land-based lines of communications. Furthermore, the Hejaz's geographical position along the east bank of the critical line of communications to the East that passed through the Red Sea

The Anglo-Hashemite Conspiracy

would give whoever was able to take advantage of its position a significant strategic asset. It is clear that Hussein concluded rather quickly that he would not automatically align himself with the sultan as he was expected to do and, indeed, was committed to do by the very terms of his appointment as sherif. Instead, he saw himself in a position to strike a bargain with the highest bidder for his allegiance. Hussein, however, was by his very nature a cautious man, and unwilling to act precipitously. It was necessary to sound out the British unobtrusively, so as not further to strain his relations with the Young Turks unnecessarily.

Thus it happened that, in February 1914, Abdullah arrived in Cairo en route between Mecca and Constantinople and paid a courtesy call on General Kitchener, the resident British agent. Abdullah used the occasion to describe to Kitchener the sorry state of relations between the Turks and the Arabs who were growing increasingly restive under Constantinople's heavy hand. He suggested that if the Young Turks attempted to depose his father, a revolt would most likely break out in the Hejaz. In such an event, as Kitchener reported to London, Abdullah had expressed the hope that "the British Government would not allow reinforcements to be sent by sea for the purpose of preventing the Arabs from exercising the rights which they have enjoyed from time immemorial in their own country round the holy places."[5] Kitchener was noncommittal in his response and put Abdullah off with diplomatic platitudes about Britain's traditional friendship with Turkey that might preclude any intervention in its territories. His response was predicated on the prevailing British assessment that the Arabs, who had a reputation as perhaps the most passive of the various peoples under Ottoman control, would be unlikely candidates for active collaboration with a foreign non-Muslim power against the nominal head of Islam. Furthermore, while Abdullah spoke of widespread Arab discontent, there was little tangible evidence of it except among a small minority of intellectuals. Nevertheless, Kitchener instructed Ronald Storrs, oriental secretary at the British Agency, to continue conversations with Abdullah and to probe the matter more deeply.

Abdullah felt more at ease with Storrs, who was fluent in Arabic. He went into greater detail about the political problems between his father and the Porte regarding the Hejaz, and ended by asking Storrs directly if the British would help Hussein obtain some machine guns. Storrs's response was discouraging. In fact, it was too early in the game for the British to do anything so provocative. Abdullah then proceeded to Constantinople in an unsuccessful attempt to come to terms with the Porte. On his return to Cairo in April 1914, Abdullah met with Storrs again. He indicated that the results of his negotiations with the Porte had proven unsatisfactory, and that he had been instructed by Hussein to approach Kitchener "with a view to obtaining with [sic] the British Government an agreement similar to that existing between the Amir of Afghanistan and the Government of India, in order to maintain the status quo in the Arabian peninsula and to do away with the danger of wanton Turkish aggression."[6] Once again the meeting with Storrs was inconclusive, offering little encouragement regarding British interest in a direct relationship with Hussein. The meetings, however, planted seeds that were to sprout later when the Turkish-German alliance became a reality.

When the conflict broke out in Europe in August 1914, Kitchener was appointed secretary of state for war. On September 24, in response to a suggestion by Storrs, Kitchener instructed him to determine from Abdullah whether "should present armed German influence at Constantinople coerce Sultan against his will and Sublime Porte to acts of aggression and war against Great Britain, he and his father and Arabs of Hejaz would be with us or against us."[7] What Kitchener was really asking was whether the sherif of Mecca would in fact support non-Muslim Britain against Muslim Turkey.

Hussein received Storrs's inquiry with ambivalence. Abdullah pressed him to make a favorable response, while his younger son Feisal urged that he stick with the Turks and thereby earn their gratitude. Hussein understood that there were considerable risks for him in aligning with the British. He would be branded by Turkish propaganda as a traitor to the Islamic cause led by the caliph, and their efforts to unseat him might find support among some of the Arabs. He decided to stall for time. He instructed Abdullah to send back a message which said in effect that, while he was favorably inclined to a relationship with Britain, his position as an Islamic leader made it difficult for him to abandon a position of neutrality—that is, unless adequate assurances were to be forthcoming. The message that arrived in Cairo on October 30 declared that "the people of the Hedjaz will accept and be well satisfied with more close union with Great Britain . . . so long as she protects the rights of our country and the rights of the person of His Highness our present Emir and Lord . . . and so long as it supports us against any foreign aggression, and in particular against the Ottomans, especially if they wish to set up anyone else as Emir."[8]

While the possibility of an Arab uprising against the Turks would have been beneficial as a means of weakening the Turkish war machine, it was by no means critical to the British as an element in their war planning. Of far greater importance was the potential for using the sherif of Mecca as a means of offsetting and discrediting a Turkish call for a holy war that might arouse the Muslim masses of India and the Nile basin.[9] Kitchener telegraphed a response the following day for delivery to Abdullah which announced Turkey's entry into the war on the side of Germany. It explicitly offered a British guarantee of Hussein's position as sherif and the defense of the Hejaz. Also, in a blatant appeal to Hussein's personal ambitions, it hinted that Britain would lend its support to Hussein's future candidacy for the highest position in Islam, the caliphate. As Kitchener put it, "It may be that an Arab of true race will assume the Khalifate at Mecca or Medina, and so good may come by the help of God out of all the evil that is now occurring." Finally, it stated, "If the Arab nation assist England in this war . . . England will . . . give Arabs every assistance against external foreign aggression."[10] In transmitting this message to Abdullah, Storrs, on his own initiative, amplified its contents in a manner that implied an unauthorized commitment of support to the liberation of the Arabs generally from Turkish rule, providing they allied themselves with England. He suggested that now, "the cause of the Arabs, which is the cause of freedom, has become the cause also of Great Britain."[11] This tendency on the part of British officials to employ rhetorical flourishes, rather than more precise diplomatic formulations, in communicating with the Arabs caused a great many unnecessary and highly troublesome misperceptions regarding British intentions in the region. In fact, it caused problems within the British government itself. The India Office agreed that the logical outcome of Arab control over the Muslim holy cities would be an Arab caliphate. However, they disagreed about the desirability of a such a course of events for British interests. According to one official of the India Office, "What we want is not a United Arabia: but a weak and disunited Arabia, split up into little principalities so far as possible under our suzerainty—but incapable of co-ordinated action against us, forming a buffer against the Powers in the West."[12]

The message was received by Abdullah on November 16 with jubilation. It was exactly what he had hoped for. Not only did it guarantee the security of both the Hejaz and the Hashemites, it also held out the possiblility of British support for a more general liberation of the Arabs from Turkish rule that would be carried out under the Hashemite banner. Hussein had Abdullah send a response back to Cairo which affirmed his secret support of Britain. However, he once again hedged about committing himself to any overt action until he was fully prepared to face the consequences of an open break with Turkey. He also sent Feisal to Constantinople via Damascus on a double mission. On the one hand, he was to determine the extent to which Arab dissatisfaction with the Ottomans in Syria might be translated into effective opposition. At the same time, he was also to explore whether there was any serious possibility of receiving tangible compensation from the Porte for his continued loyalty. In the interim, Hussein continued to make the most of his current situation by means of a duplicitous cooperation with German efforts to undermine the British position in the Middle East.

According to German foreign ministry documents, the Germans had made contact with both Hussein in the Hejaz and his archrival Ibn Saud in Nejd, seeking their support against the British. A headquarters for revolutionary activity in the region was established in Damascus which was linked to the German consulates in both Medina and Jeddah. The Germans reached an understanding with Hussein under which, for regular payments, the sherif would facilitate the dissemination of German anti-British propaganda in the territories under his control, in addition to other unspecified activities. The last payments listed in the German records were made in June 1915.[13] Interestingly, there thus appears to have been a brief period of overlap when Hussein was being compensated for services by both the Germans and the British.

As the British had anticipated, once Turkey entered the war, the sultan promptly tried to capitalize on his role as caliph to rouse the Muslims as a body against the Entente Powers. He called for a holy war. On November 7, the shaikh al-Islam, the highest religious official in the Ottoman Empire, issued a formal pronouncement that declared it to be the sacred personal duty of every Muslim to rise against Britain, France and Russia, all of which were now designated as enemies of Islam. Then, on November 11, the sultan issued a proclamation to the armed forces charging them with the mission of liberating all Muslims from subservience to the governments of the Entente. Finally, on November 23, a manifesto, signed by the shaikh al-Islam and twenty-eight other religious dignitaries, was issued to the Muslim world calling upon all Muslims to participate in the defense of Islam and the holy places. These formal steps were followed up by a massive barrage of supportive propaganda calculated to appeal to the masses of the common people. A horde of itinerant preachers, teachers and agitators descended on virtually every nook and cranny of the Muslim world, carrying the sultan's message. A particular emphasis was placed on agitation among the Arabs, because it was they who were best positioned geographically to harass the flanks of the Entente Powers, especially Britain.[14]

Kitchener's message of October 31 reached Hussein at about the same time as the sultan's call to join him in the holy war. Hussein stalled the Turks by arguing that while he prayed for the success of the jihad, it was impossible for him to join it actively at that time. The British were in control of the Red Sea and were therefore positioned to blockade the Hejaz ports, cutting off the import of any supplies, including food. Should food supplies run out, there was grave danger of a revolt against the sherif which would further weaken the Turkish position in Arabia and work to the advantage of the British. Therefore, until the supply lines to the Hejaz could be assured of adequate protection, he could not run the risk of a British blockade, nor was it in the Porte's interest that he do so. Hussein stuck by this argument, and the Turks had no real choice but to accept it. However, they were not deceived by it, notwithstanding its plausibility. They soon began to plot Hussein's removal and replacement by a more accommodating sherif. Hussein understood that his personal future within the Ottoman imperial framework was becoming increasingly gloomy, unless he could do something dramatic to redeem himself in Turkish eyes.

At the end of January 1915, an emissary from the Arab nationalist leaders in Syria and Iraq arrived in Mecca with an invitation for Hussein to assume the leadership of a revolt intended to achieve Arab independence from the Turks. Since Hussein already had a reputation for standing up to the Turks, the nationalists hoped to use his name and position as a rallying point to compensate for their own obscurity. It must remain doubtful that they ever really considered Hussein, or either of his sons afterward, as anything more than a useful figurehead. It was at this point that Feisal was sent on his mission to Damascus and Constantinople to assess the state of affairs. Feisal arrived in Damascus on March 26, and spent a month there feeling out how serious the Arab nationalists were and whether they were capable of implementing the planned revolt. He discovered that the main factor inhibiting the outbreak of an Arab nationalist revolt was the fear of British, French, Italian and Russian ambitions in the Middle East. It made little sense to the nationalists to throw off the Muslim Turkish yoke in order to be swallowed up by the Christian Europeans. Feisal personally shared their misgivings, which was the basic reason for his disagreement with Abdullah over whether to join forces with the British.

After his inconclusive visit to Constantinople, Feisal returned to Damascus on May 23 to find that the leaders of the Arab nationalist societies had drawn up a protocol which defined the terms they demanded as a condition for undertaking a revolt against the Turks and in support of the Entente. The protocol called for:

- The recognition by Great Britain of the independence of the Arab countries lying within the following frontiers: north—the line Mersin-Adana to parallel 37N and thence along the line Birejik-Urfa-Mardin-Midiat-Jazirat (Ibn 'Umar)-Amadia to the Persian frontier; east—the

Persian frontier down to the Persian Gulf; south—the Indian Ocean (with the exclusion of Aden, whose status was to be maintained); and west—the Red Sea and the Mediterranean back to Mersin.
- The abolition of all exceptional privileges granted to foreigners under the Capitulations.
- The conclusion of a defensive alliance between Great Britain and the future independent Arab state.
- The grant of economic preference to Great Britain.[15]

It was the Arab leaders' view that only if the Entente Powers agreed to a specific commitment that would result in a sovereign Arab state, would it be worth the risks of a revolt against the Turks, who were certain to attempt to suppress it with great brutality. Feisal told them that he did not believe that the British and French would accept these terms, although he agreed that they represented the minimum commitments that would justify a revolt.

Feisal returned to Mecca on June 20 and briefed Hussein exhaustively regarding his discussions in both Damascus and Constantinople. After considering Feisal's report, Hussein decided to make an offer of Arab allegiance to the British based on the terms of the Damascus protocol, plus a requirement for a definite commitment of support from Britain to his candidacy for the caliphate as originally hinted at by Kitchener. Hussein's unsigned and undated letter to Sir Henry McMahon, the British high commissioner in Egypt, was enclosed in a personal letter from Abdullah to Storrs, dated July 14, 1915.

McMahon was taken aback by the audacity of the Arab demands. He had already informed the foreign secretary, Sir Edward Grey, that with regard to his negotiations with the Arabs, the term "independent Sovereign State has been interpreted in a generic sense because the idea of an Arabian unity under one ruler, recognized as supreme by other Arab chiefs, is as yet inconceivable to the Arab mind."[16] Ronald Storrs, who stayed on as oriental secretary after Kitchener's departure, commented that upon seeing Hussein's note, "We could not conceal from ourselves (and with difficulty from him) that his pretensions bordered upon the tragi-comic."[17] For one thing, the demand for the full independence of the vast region indicated in the Damascus protocol was grossly inconsistent with Anglo-French ideas about the future of Syria and Mesopotamia. Furthermore, there was substantial doubt about how significant an Arab uprising would be in any case, in terms of the overall war effort, to justify such far-reaching political commitments on the part of Britain. Accordingly, McMahon's response of August 30 included a mere reaffirmation of British support for the liberation of the Arabs from Turkish rule and a more positive commitment regarding the caliphate. With regard to the territorial demands, McMahon argued that "negotiations would appear to be premature and a waste of time on details at this stage, with the War in progress and the Turks in effective occupation of the greater part of those regions."[18] He noted further that, at the time, the Arabs were in fact assisting the Turks and Germans, rather than demonstrating their opposition.

As anticipated, the evasive British reply did not satisfy Hussein. On September 9, he wrote to McMahon again demanding clarification of Britain's position on the question of the Arab territories. "The fact is that the proposed frontiers and boundaries represent not the suggestions of one individual whose claim might well await the conclusion of the War, but the demands of our people who believe that those frontiers form the minimum necessary to the establishment of the new order for which they are striving. This they are determined to obtain."

It took more than a month for the British to formulate a reply. What McMahon finally transmitted to Hussein regarding the nature and extent of the British commitment to Arab territorial ambitions has ever since been a subject of intense controversy. In essence, McMahon's second letter to Hussein of October 24 accepted the frontiers of the Damascus protocol with some significant exceptions. McMahon stated: "The districts of Mersin and Alexandretta, and portions of Syria lying to the west of the districts of Damascus, Homs, Hama and Aleppo, cannot be said to be purely Arab, and must on that account be excepted from the proposed delimitation."

Hussein had won a major political victory. In his response to McMahon of November 5, he conceded the British point regarding Mersin and Adana. However, with regard to the "vilayets of Aleppo and Bairut and their western maritime coasts," he insisted that "these are purely Arab provinces in which the Moslem is indistinguishable from the Christian, for they are both the descendants of one forefather." Significantly absent from this correspondence was any mention of the Jews of Palestine, a factor that Hussein would be forced to take cognizance of later. From the British perspective, Palestine could readily be considered as falling within their expressed reservation regarding the areas that "cannot be said to be purely Arab, and must on that account be excepted from the proposed delimitation." What Hussein obviously did not realize was that at the same time that the British were negotiating for his support, a similar effort was being directed toward the Jews. The latter also had territorial interests and aspirations in the region, and were busily engaged in building settlements within the vilayet of Beirut, which included the sanjaks of Beirut, Acre and Balqa—that is, the northern half of Palestine.

The Government of India remained adamantly opposed to supporting an Arab revolt in Mesopotamia, which it continued to view as inimical to Britain's interests. Its position was perhaps best articulated by Sir Arthur Hirtzel in an internal India Office memorandum. He wrote:

> A strong Arab State might be more dangerous to Christendom than a strong Ottoman State, & Lord Kitchener's policy of destroying one Islamic State merely for the purpose of creating another, has always seemed to me disastrous, from the point of view no less of expediency than of civilisation. The justification of the policy of H.M.G. lies mainly in the fact that the Arabs have shown themselves incapable of creating or maintaining such a State; &, inasmuch as it will be to the joint interests of France, Russia & ourselves to prevent them from doing so in fact—while enabling them to present a suitable facade to the world—the policy is probably also sufficiently free from practical danger. The danger of it, to my mind, lies in its disingenuousness."[19]

Interestingly, one of the main supporters of the agreement with Hussein, Sir Reginald Wingate, who replaced McMahon as high commissioner in Egypt, saw Britain as being in an essentially no-lose position. He inquired of Gilbert Clayton in a private note in November 1915: "What harm can our acceptance of his proposals do? If the embryonic Arab state comes to nothing, all our promises vanish and we are absolved from them—if the Arab state becomes a reality, we have quite sufficient safe-guards to control it and although eventually it might act towards its "Allied" creators as Bulgaria has acted towards Russia—I think it is within our power to erect such barriers as would effectively prevent its becoming a menace, which the Indian Government appears to fear."[20]

The secretary of state for India, Austen Chamberlain, recognizing that the government was compelled to abide by the unwarranted and unprecedented commitment that McMahon had made on his own initiative, harbored great doubts about Hussein's credibility as a leader. He noted that "my information is that the Grand Shareef is a nonentity without power to carry out his proposals." Accordingly, he insisted in his memorandum of November 8, 1915, to the Foreign Office that "the next step should be to make clear to them that promises made by McMahon are dependent on immediate action by them in sense of their offers and will not be binding on us unless they do their part at once."[21]

McMahon's third note to Hussein on December 17 reflected the intense pressure he was under as a consequence of his earlier commitments. Echoing Chamberlain's adamant position, he now insisted that Hussein begin to make good on his promises. He wrote: "It is most essential that you spare no effort to attach all the Arab peoples to our united cause and urge them to afford no assistance to our enemies. It is on the success of these efforts and on the more active measures which the Arabs may thereafter take in support of our cause, when the time for action comes, that the permanence and strength of our agreement must depend."[22] He then also pointed out that there were French interests involved in the vilayets of Beirut and Aleppo, and that Britain could not negotiate those interests with him on behalf of France. Detailed negotiations with the French, that were to culminate in the Sykes-Picot Agreement, had begun in December 1915. While Hussein had not been formally told of the negotiations, he had been kept informally aware of the Anglo-French discussions by Muhammad al-Faruqi, who served as an intermediary between Mecca and Cairo. Detecting the clear change of tone in McMahon's latest communication, Hussein saw no value in attempting to force the British into further concessions on Syria. He decided to

The Anglo-Hashemite Conspiracy

defer the matter for the moment. However, in his reply to McMahon of January 1, 1916, he reserved the right to reaffirm his claim to the Beirut region after the war was concluded. McMahon, in his final note of January 30, acknowledged Hussein's reservation and extended his appreciation for the emir's readiness to defer those demands that would have a negative effect on Anglo-French relations while the war was in progress.

To gain some further insight about what all this meant to the British at the time, it is worth noting Clayton's explicit denial on March 11, 1916 (he was then director of military intelligence in Cairo) that it was McMahon's intention to promote "the establishment of a powerful Arab Kingdom. . . . All we want is to keep the friendship and, if possible, the active assistance of the various Arab chiefs . . . while at the same time, working towards maintenance of the *status quo ante bellum,* and merely eliminating Turkish domination from Arabia." On April 17, 1916, Clayton wrote again that "to set up a great Arab State . . . was never my idea. . . . The conditions throughout Arabia, Syria and Mesopotamia did not allow of such a scheme being practical, even if anyone were so foolish as to attempt it. . . . The object we have to aim at is, I consider, to work to preserve all the various elements in the Arab territories very much in the same position as they were before the war, but minus the Turks. In this way we shall have an open field to work in."[23] The Hussein-McMahon correspondence thus meant significantly different things to the different parties involved. Arnold Toynbee, then of the Arab Bureau, pointed out their deficiencies as a basis for Anglo-Arab relations:

> Our commitments to King Hussein are not embodied in any agreement or treaty or even acknowledged by both parties. In this way they differ from those to Russia, France, Italy and certain independent Arab rulers such as the Idrisi and Bin Saud. They can only be analysed by summarizing the history of our dealings with the King during the War, under different heads. And the position is complicated by the King's habit of ignoring or refusing to take note of conditions laid down by us to which he objects and then carrying on as if the particular question had been settled between us according to his own desires."[24]

While these negotiations with Britain were in progress for more than half a year, Hussein was simultaneously conducting negotiations with the Turks in an effort to obtain a commitment of support for continued Hashemite rule in the Hejaz. In September 1915, Feisal, who was much disposed to finding a way to reach an accommodation with the Turks, was dispatched to Constantinople to render assurances of Hussein's continuing loyalty to the Porte. The Porte, however, was not sufficiently forthcoming with regard to the assurances sought by Hussein. Feisal left the Ottoman capital with little recourse but to help prepare the now seemingly inevitable Arab revolt. He then returned to Damascus in early January 1916 for the purpose of fomenting a revolt by the Arab divisions in the Turkish army upon a signal from Hussein.[25]

When McMahon's final note arrived in Mecca, Hussein nonetheless decided to try once more to obtain a guarantee of his position from the Turks. In February 1916 he telegraphed Constantinople and demanded immediate assurances regarding the hereditary claims of the Hashemites to Hejaz. Once again, the desired assurances were not forthcoming. Instead, he was informed by Djemal Pasha, a member of the ruling triumvirate of the Committee of Union and Progress and de facto dictator of Syria and Palestine, that at the beginning of April a Turkish force of some 3,500 picked and specially equipped troops was going to march through the Hejaz en route to Yemen. Hussein suspected that the Turks might have something else in mind, and was determined to prevent any bolstering of the Turkish garrison in Arabia, especially at a time when he was thinking about leading a revolt against them. Accordingly, his loyal Bedouin troops surrounded Medina, cutting off the Turkish garrison there from supplies and reinforcements. Feisal, who was still in Damascus at the time, was nonplussed by his father's seemingly impulsive step. Confronted by Djemal, Feisal had to convince him that he and the Hashemites were not traitors to the sultan. According to Djemal, he protested, "How could we be traitors, members of a family descended from the Prophet, a family whose greatest honor it is to be the most devoted and loyal followers of the Khalif."[26]

At about the same time, the Turkish authorities in Syria began a roundup of Arab notables suspected of involvement in the independence movement. On May 6, twenty-one of them were

The Anglo-Hashemite Conspiracy

summarily executed in Damascus and Beirut for "treasonable participation in activities of which the aims were to separate Syria, Palestine and Iraq from the Ottoman Sultanate and to constitute them into an independent State."[27] At this point it became quite clear to Hussein that there was no longer any real hope of reaching any true accommodation with the Turks. He decided to act. But first he had to get Feisal out of Turkish hands.

Within a few days, Feisal received a secretly delivered message to return to Mecca as soon as possible. He managed to convince Djemal that Hussein, as a demonstration of his loyalty to the Porte, had raised an expeditionary force of Bedouin warriors that was to be placed at the disposal of the Turkish army. It was now necessary for Feisal to return to the Hejaz in order to lead this Bedouin force back to Damascus to join Djemal's Fourth Turkish Army. According to Djemal, Feisal went so far as to swear "by the glorious soul of the Prophet to return at an early date at the head of his warriors" to help "fight the infidels to the death."[28] Djemal was apparently convinced by Feisal's story and allowed him to leave Damascus on May 16. Needless to say, it was the last that Djemal ever saw of him. As soon as Feisal was safely back a few weeks later, in June 1916, Hussein gave the signal to begin the Arab revolt.

The revolt met with a number of initial successes in the Hejaz, where Hussein's influence was strongest. By the end of the summer of 1916, the relatively small Turkish military presence along the Arabian Red Sea coast was virtually eliminated. This was potentially significant for the war effort in that it precluded the use of the Hejaz coast for the refueling of German submarines preying on traffic through the Suez Canal. However, after this accomplishment, the revolt soon seemed to run out of steam. Within a few weeks, the British sponsors of the Hussein connection were not only embarrassed by the fact that nothing of any particular significance was happening on the Arab front, they were actually concerned that the whole enterprise might prove counterproductive, as predicted by its opponents in the India Office. Aside from the coast, the Turks held fast to their positions in the Hejaz, including Medina and the important rail terminal there. Before the revolt started, the British were led to believe that Hussein could rally a force of a quarter million Arabs to his banner. It was soon evident, however, that the most he could actually muster as a reliable force was between three and four thousand tribesmen. By July 9, McMahon was pleading with London for military assistance to cut off the Turks and "prevent early collapse of Sherif's movement."[29] The revolt also failed to inspire a general Arab uprising against the Turks in Syria and Mesopotamia. Indeed, even in the Arabian peninsula, the Hashemites failed to gain the allegiance of the tribal leaders outside the Harb Confederation. Particularly disappointing was the fact that the tribes near Medina, in Hussein's own backyard, remained loyal to the sultan throughout the war. The Mesopotamian and Palestinian Arabs remained placid throughout the war, and nothing happened in Syria until Hussein's forces entered Palestine the following year. As for the Arab troops raised by Hussein and Feisal, it was only after British officers took over the planning and de facto direction of the Arab war effort that they became a credible force, capable of harassing the Turkish lines of communication.

Notwithstanding the sorry state of the Arab revolt, on October 30, 1916, having been led by his advisers to believe that what he was about to do reflected his mutual understanding with the British, Hussein declared himself king of the Arabs. Shocked by Hussein's audacity, if not arrogance, McMahon, anticipating another barrage of criticism for this latest act of folly, quickly wrote to the Foreign Office in self-vindication, explaining,

> Whatever references the Sherif may make to terms and expressions used in previous, and what would appear to be imaginary, communications, the records of our correspondence will, I am sure, prove not only that we have abstained from saying anything that implies the future existence of any supreme ruler in Arabia, but also that geographical terms that in English may have been loosely expressed by such words as Country, Kingdom, Empire etc., have in the Arabic version been expressed by the interchange of such words as "mamlakah", "doulah", and "hukumah" none of which necessarily imply the existence of a king. Also in certain passages the term Arab Government has been expressed in the plural.[30]

Both Britain and France objected strenuously to Hussein's arrogation of authority to speak for the Arabs, and resolved to accord him recognition only as king of Hejaz. From Hussein's perspective, however, this challenge to his status was both unreasonable and inconsistent with what he understood to be Britain's far-reaching commitments to him. He had been encouraged by the British quite explicitly to consider himself as the future caliph of Islam. Since the caliphate was currently occupied by the sultan, it was only appropriate that the sultan of the Turks should be replaced in that exalted position by the king of the Arabs. To become caliph therefore meant to become king of the Arabs as a first step. It was quite evident that Hussein was primarily motivated by a vain ambition to build a dynastic Hashemite empire to replace the Ottoman. The matter of Arab nationalism per se was a secondary if not lower-order consideration. The fervor that might be generated by Hussein's support of an ill-defined notion of Arab nationalism would be yoked to the Hashemite banner, to serve as an instrument for fulfilling Hussein's dreams of empire. T. E. Lawrence, who would later, and for reasons unrelated to any concern with the legitimacy of Hashemite goals and ambitions, glorify the Arab revolt, had few if any illusions about the strength and character of Arab nationalism during the period in which it emerged, or about Hussein's ability to forge an Arab national state. In a November 1916 report, he wrote to Cairo: "Their ideas of nationality is the independence of tribes and parishes and their idea of national union is episodic, combined resistance to an intruder. Constructive politics, an organized state, and an extensive empire are not only beyond their capacity, but anathema to their instincts. . . . Unless we, or our Allies, make an efficient Arab empire, there will never be more than a discordant mosaic of provisional administrations."[31]

Furthermore, from the British perspective, Hussein's self-proclaimed importance was hardly commensurate with his actual strength and contribution to the defeat of the Turkish enemy. In the fall of 1916, the Turks recovered from their initial shock at the Arab revolt. They were determined to retake Mecca and replace Hussein as sherif with someone more reliable. By December 1916, after the Turks had taken to the offensive and seemed likely to recapture Rabegh in their drive toward Medina, Hussein's forces began to dissipate as a consequence of the extensive desertions that were taking place. Hussein, however, preferred to place the blame for his difficulties on the British, suggesting that the problem was inadequate British support of the Arab war effort. At one point, Feisal went so far as to threaten to enter into peace negotiations with the Turks unless increased material support was forthcoming.[32] Since the British had already supplied Hussein's army with more than fifty thousand rifles and appropriate quantities of ammunition, they understood this demand to be one for an increase in Hussein's cash subsidy. Apologists will of course suggest that this was merely a tactic employed by Feisal to force British concessions at a critical point. It may indeed have been such. However, Feisal could not have been unaware of the impression it would create regarding the sincerity of the Hashemite commitment to the nationalist struggle against the Ottomans.

In May 1917, Mark Sykes and Georges Picot went to Jeddah to meet with Hussein. They reported to him generally regarding the arrangement they had concluded that would place certain of the territories to be liberated from the Ottomans under British or French supervision. Later, Muhammad Rashid Rida was to write:

> There came to Cairo in [April–May 1917] one of the Arab leaders who were with the Amir Faisal. We found him convinced that the King had agreed with the English and the French over their plans for Syria and Iraq. I again heard the same story a month later from another Muslim who was connected with the secret societies. Others who were in Amir Faisal's entourage have informed us that they saw a letter from his father to him, mentioning the same thing and giving as a reason for his consent that France would guard the Syrian coast for him until the Arab state could acquire a navy capable of defending it, and that France would pay a stipulated sum to the Arab state every year so long as she occupied the coast.[33]

During the early part of 1917, from his headquarters at Wejh in the Hejaz, Feisal concentrated on building up his forces and broadening his power base among the Bedouin tribes of northern Hejaz and Transjordan. His army of some six hundred men was estimated to have been augmented by between twenty to twenty-five thousand ill-disciplined Bedouin irregulars. One of the more significant Bedouin additions to his alliance was Auda Abu Tayeh, the chief of the Tawayha branch of the Huwaitat tribal confederation.

The Anglo-Hashemite Conspiracy

Auda proposed an audacious surprise attack on the Turkish-held and strategically important port of Aqaba, an attack which he successfully carried out during the first week of July. The new British commander, General Allenby, was impressed by the unanticipated success of the attack on Aqaba and decided to make greater tactical use of Hussein's forces to create diversions on the British right flank. Large quantities of additional war supplies soon began flowing to the Arab forces through the recently captured Red Sea port.

However, it was soon made clear once again that the professions of Arab nationalist fervor had failed to strike deep roots among the Hashemites and their followers. For some of the principal Arab leaders the ultimate success of the struggle against the Turks was at best a secondary concern. In August 1917 it was discovered that Auda had been in contact with the Turks, who were trying to negotiate a deal with him that would lead to his defection from Feisal's camp. When confronted by Lawrence with evidence of this perfidy, Auda responded by threatening to hand Aqaba back to the Turks unless he received a larger share of the booty.[34] Since the Turks were putting up a very stiff resistance to the British advance through Palestine and Allenby needed whatever help the Arabs might provide, it was decided to accommodate Auda's demands; the subsidy to Hussein was enlarged once more. At the same time, it appears that Hussein harbored some resentment regarding the role assigned to his forces by the British, which placed them in a subordinate but nonetheless precarious position. The capture of Aqaba meant in effect that the Hejaz was secure, notwithstanding the Turkish garrison at Medina. This was Hussein's primary concern. It was unclear that he was really committed to endangering his slim army to defeat the Turks in Palestine and Syria. As noted by Richard Aldington in his definitive debunking of the myth of the Arab revolt created and popularized by Lawrence, Feisal's forces preferred to remain in the "desert areas close to the British army, from which small raids could be made with comparative immunity. Beyond those areas, where there was real danger to be found and real damage to be done, the Arabs did nothing but talk and conspire."[35]

The serious problems of motivation and morale in the Arab army soon became evident to Allenby. With the advance of the British forces north from Egypt and the defeat of the Turks in Sinai, Allenby was positioned for a drive through Palestine into Syria. However, the determination of the Turks to block the British advance in Palestine was greater than had been anticipated. By April 1917 the British offensive ground to a halt in front of Gaza, where it remained bogged down for a year. In January and February 1918, as the British prepared to break through the Gaza bottleneck, the Arab forces were charged by Allenby with the capture of the Jordan Valley and the severing of the Turkish supply lines to the main front. Their efforts were not very successful, however, and the Arabs were distressed by their losses. Hussein's youngest son, Zeid, refused to continue the campaign unless the British supplied more money. As the British and Arab forces pushed further northward in the spring of 1918, the Turkish resistance became more dogged. In the face of the increasing Turkish determination to hold the line, the Arab offensive slowed and then dissipated. When Allenby took advantage of an opportunity created through a diversionary action to cross the Jordan River and seize Amman, a critical situation developed. The British forces holding the city did so with the expectation that there would be a simultaneous Arab offensive in the Jordan Valley designed to relieve the Turkish pressure on Allenby's overextended lines of communication. However, when Feisal's forces attacked Ma'an, they were repulsed with heavy losses. Subsequent attempts to cut the Turkish lines of communication also failed to provide the necessary relief. For three months the British urged the Arabs to mount a new offensive. When none materialized, Allenby's forces were compelled to abandon Amman.

That same summer, Feisal once again toyed with the idea of abandoning the British in exchange for a Turkish evacuation of Amman, which would then be turned over to Hussein. It appears that he was prepared to settle for an enlargement of the Hashemite kingdom of Hejaz to include Transjordan. When Lawrence learned that Feisal was in contact with a representative of Djemal, he sent Hussein a clear warning not to betray Britain. Hussein vigorously denied the accusation of double dealing, and

The Anglo-Hashemite Conspiracy

Feisal ceased his negotiations. Hussein's forces played virtually no further role in the Middle East fighting until near the very end of the war in the region. Then, facing almost no opposition as the Turkish front collapsed. Feisal resumed his advance through Transjordan toward Damascus, which fell on October 1, 1918.

As the war in the Middle East moved toward a conclusion, the British began to focus increasingly on the agreements concerning the division of the spoils worked out earlier with the French. In particular, as stated poignantly in the British Cabinet by Lord Milner, they wanted "to diddle the French out of Syria."[36] The only predictable way of doing this was to establish an acceptably plausible Arab claim to the country. Accordingly, the British had begun preparing the basis for such a claim in the spring of 1918. At that time, a group of seven Arab notables living in Cairo decided to request clarification from the British government regarding its policies for the region in the postwar period. The request was precipitated by the general confusion that resulted from the apparent inconsistencies between the McMahon commitments to Hussein, the Sykes-Picot Agreement, which had now become publicly known, and the Balfour Declaration (see the next chapter). The query was transmitted to the Foreign Office through the Arab Bureau in Cairo. The official government response, which was given to the group of seven on June 16, subsequently became known as the Declaration to the Seven. In that response, the British government, in specific reference to "Territories liberated from Turkish rule by the *action of the Arabs themselves,*" committed itself to "recognize the complete and sovereign independence of the Arabs inhabiting those territories, and support them in their struggle for freedom."[37]

With this unambiguous commitment in hand, the British, most notably Lawrence working in conjunction with Feisal, conspired to arrange for the *Arab liberation* of Syria. The procedure that was followed has been described by the Arab historian Muhammad Kurd Ali: "Wherever the British Army captured a town or reduced a fortress which was to be given to the Arabs it would halt until the Arabs could enter, and the capture would be credited to them."[38] Matters became somewhat more complicated with regard to the conquest of Damascus. Allenby, as the commander-in-chief of the Allied armies, had ordered the British as well as

French and Australian forces driving the Turks from Damascus to stop their advance outside the city. In this way, Feisal would be allowed to enter the city first with his Arab forces and establish a provisional government. The plan was predicated on the assumption that the Turkish forces in the city were completely cut off from any retreat, and would therefore have no alternative but to surrender to Feisal. However, this fundamental assumption turned out to be fallacious. The Australian commander, Brigadier Wilson, discovered that he could not complete the envelopment of the Turkish forces without entering the city first. That he did, out of military necessity, and the Turkish commander surrendered the city to him rather than to Feisal, who had not yet entered Damascus.[39] Nonetheless, the British promoted the fiction of the Arab capture of Damascus, and allowed Feisal to set up an administration there.

2

The Anglo-Zionist Conspiracy

Toward the end of the nineteenth century, Theodor Herzl, founder of the modern political Zionist movement, set about almost single-handedly to reestablish a Jewish national state in the land of biblical Israel. While there had been an earlier resurgence of Jewish national feeling that had brought about the slow but steady development of Jewish settlements in Palestine, the process was too incremental and problematic for Herzl. He was convinced that the idea of the reestablishment of the Jewish national entity could best be realized through dramatic political action. Since the Ottoman Empire was ridden with corruption and was on the brink of insolvency, he believed that a desirable accommodation could be reached with the sultan, who was desperately in need of financial assistance.

Accordingly, in 1896, through a third party with good access to the Ottoman court in Constantinople, Herzl proposed to the sultan that the Jews be given the land of Palestine for the purpose of establishing an independent Jewish republic there. In return, Herzl offered the mobilization of sufficient Jewish financial resources to restore Turkey's fiscal health. The sultan might have been prepared to conclude an arrangement with the Zionists to allow colonization. He would not, however, agree to a cession of territory. According to P. M. Nevlinski, Herzl's go-between to the sultan, Abdul-Hamid told him:

> If Mr. Herzl is your friend in the same measure as you are mine, then advise him not to go a single step further in the matter. I cannot sell even a foot of land, for it does not belong to me but to my people. They have won this Empire and fertilized it with their blood. We will cover it once more with our blood, before we allow it to be torn from us. . . . The Turkish people own the Turkish Empire, not I. I can dispose of no part of it. The Jews may spare their millions. When my Empire is divided, perhaps they will get Palestine for nothing. But only our corpse can be divided, I will never consent to vivisection.[1]

Nonetheless, Herzl was convinced that the sultan could be won over, that he was merely holding out for a better offer. As events were to prove, Herzl's optimism was not well founded.

The following year, the First Zionist Congress, meeting in Basel, Switzerland, in a formula devised by Max Nordau that deliberately obscured what Herzl was quite clear about, declared, "The object of Zionism is the establishment for the Jewish people of a home in Palestine secured by public law."[2] The purpose of this formulation was twofold. First, by not speaking explicitly in terms of a state, the Zionist program gained greater acceptance among Jews who were troubled by Herzl's more explicit goal of a sovereign Jewish political entity. Only recently emancipated in most of Europe, many Jews were understandably concerned about how Herzl's ideas would be viewed by the governments of their countries of domicile. There was widespread fear that the advocacy of Jewish nationalism would raise the issue of dual loyalty, a charge that could severely damage Jewish communal interests as well as the status of the individual Jew. Second, given the position taken by the sultan regarding the cession of Turkish-held land in Palestine, it was considered prudent to cast the Zionist goal in terms that would not further aggravate the Turks, upon whose cooperation the success of the Zionist enterprise largely depended. However, it was as clear then as it has been since that this formulation was nothing but an obfuscating euphemism for a Jewish national state. Only the naive or ignorant could possibly have believed otherwise.

The Anglo-Zionist Conspiracy

Under Herzl's leadership, the nationalist movement accorded highest priority to achieving political recognition of Zionism's aspirations. With his death in 1904, however, the Zionist leadership began to adopt a somewhat different approach. At the Tenth Zionist Congress in August 1911, "political" Zionism took second place to "practical" Zionism. This latter approach was one that sought to achieve Zionist aspirations by creating and shaping tangible reality in a way that could lead toward no other end than Herzl's Jewish state. This meant a focus on colonization and the building of a communal infrastructure in Palestine itself. If, in order to appease the Turkish government, it was necessary to disavow any desire for national independence—so be it. The president of the Zionist Organization thus declared: "The aim of Zionism is the erection for the Jewish people of a publicly recognized, legally secure home in Palestine. Not a Jewish state, but a home in the ancient land of our forefathers, where we can live a Jewish life without oppression and persecution. What we demand is that the Jewish immigrant to Palestine be given the opportunity of naturalizing as a citizen without limitation, and that he can live unhindered in accordance with Jewish customs."[3]

That this new formulation did not really deceive anyone regarding ultimate Zionist intentions became disturbingly evident in Palestine immediately after the outbreak of World War I. The Zionist Organization, whose members were to be found in all the belligerent countries, on both sides, necessarily adopted a position of complete neutrality. Notwithstanding the official Zionist policy, Djemal Pasha, the Turkish supreme commander in Syria and Palestine, issued special instructions for "combatting the activity of the seditious movement which is attempting, under the name of Zionism, to erect a Jewish Government in the Palestinian portion of the Ottoman Empire."[4] Djemal's perception of the political implications of Zionist colonization was buttressed by that of Baha ad-Din Bey, the former commissioner for Jewish affairs in Palestine at the Porte, who was now governor of Jaffa. In a detailed report, he gave the following description of the character of Zionist colonization:

> The attempt of the Jews to separate themselves from the rest of the inhabitants; their retention of foreign nationality; their submission of

litigation to Jewish courts . . . their own symbols of statehood, in particular the blue and white flag . . . their purchase of land in an attempt to possess themselves of the country; their disrespect of Turkish authority and of the Turkish language in schools which inculcate Jewish nationalist and anti-Turkish sentiment; and the autonomy of the Jewish colonies, with their own law courts and defense services.[5]

There was indeed much truth to this characterization of Zionist activity in Palestine. The Zionist Yishuv (settlement) was fully intent on building autonomous Jewish structures in Palestine that would provide the basis for an ultimately independent Jewish state as originally envisaged by Herzl. They surely placed little value on Turkish institutions or authority, which were afflicted by the universally deplored corruption for which the Porte had become infamous. And, indeed, most of the Jews who had settled in Palestine before the outbreak of the war had not applied for Ottoman citizenship. It was beyond question that they had greater assurance of physical security by retaining the nationality of their countries of origin. They thus preferred to rely on the intervention on their behalf by the European consulates that wielded considerable authority under the Capitulations that had been imposed on the Ottoman Empire by the European powers.

The onset of the war placed the Zionists, and most particularly the Zionist settlers in Palestine, in a quandary. As noted, there were large numbers of Jews residing in the countries of the opposing sides. This argued for the neutrality adopted by the Zionist Organization. On the other hand, such a stance on the part of the Yishuv would be seen as treasonous by the Turkish authorities. An example of what was to be expected was given by Baha-ad-din in December 1914, when he ordered the expulsion of all Jewish foreign nationals on the seventeenth of that month.[6] The order created a storm of protest and precipitated the political intervention of the German government, Turkey's ally. The order was reversed, but not in time to avoid the expulsion of some six thousand Russian Jews residing in Jaffa. This led to a major naturalization campaign in the country to avoid destruction of the community. Some Jewish officials, including David Ben-Gurion and Yitzhak Ben-Zvi, attempted to go even further in demonstrating their commitment to the support of Turkey and petitioned for the authority to establish a Jewish militia to help defend the country.[7]

Notwithstanding Djemal's strong antipathy to Jewish as well as Arab nationalism, during the early war period Zionist emissaries continued to approach both the Turkish and German governments in an effort to convince them of the benefits they could derive through the support of Zionist aspirations, which continued to be portrayed in minimalist terms. The argument made to the Turks was essentially that presented by Herzl two decades earlier. Turkey would need substantial financial assistance to rebuild during the postwar period, and Zionist gratitude could help fill that need. To this was now added a new and novel argument. The current severe suppression of Arab nationalism by Djemal could not continue indefinitely. After the war, some accommodation would have to be reached on Arab autonomy within the Ottoman Empire. In this case, it could serve Turkish interests in Palestine to have any Arab nationalist ambitions there offset by the presence of a substantial autonomous Jewish community.

Describing his approach to the German Embassy in Constantinople, Richard Lichtheim wrote to an associate that he had tried every argument imaginable, including the Jewish cultural affinity with Germany which could make an autonomous Jewish presence in Palestine a significant cultural base for German interests in the Near East.[8] None of this was to any avail, and as the Turkish repression in Palestine increased, there was a notable shift of Zionist interest toward the Entente.

By early 1915, some ten thousand Jews from Palestine had been given asylum in Egypt by the British authorities. It was there that a movement to recruit a Jewish legion to fight the Turks in Palestine was inaugurated by Vladimir Jabotinsky, a Jewish journalist from Russia. Although the British indicated some interest in the idea, they preferred to limit it to a Jewish transportation unit to be assigned elsewhere for service. When it became clear that the unit was not going to serve in Palestine, Jabotinsky withdrew from the effort and continued to agitate for a Jewish legion that would fight to liberate Palestine from the Turks. This alternate proposal was accepted by the other Jewish leaders, most particularly Joseph Trumpeldor, and by April 1915 some five hundred volunteers were accepted into the Zion Mule Corps, which was to serve with distinction during the Gallipoli Campaign which concluded the following December.[9]

That same winter, the British became engaged in a series of complex negotiations with France regarding the postwar disposition of the territories of the Ottoman Empire that they had already decided to dismantle. With the French loss of the Suez Canal to the British after 1875, Syria had become a prime goal of their imperialist program of expansion in the Far East. Syria could serve as the Mediterranean terminal for an overland route to the Indian Ocean, to replace the canal. Consequently, France sought relentlessly to gain control over the ports of Syria and Palestine which could serve as rail terminals for a line linking the two bodies of water. In addition, France was concerned to maintain its naval supremacy in the Mediterranean. Toward this end, it had established a chain of naval bases along the North African littoral, and was now anxious to have an equivalent position at the Mediterranean's eastern extremity. Between 1910 and 1913, France repeatedly tried to convince the Turkish government to award it concessions for the construction of modern ports at Jaffa, Haifa and Tripoli. They already had a predominant position in Beirut. With the rise of the Arab nationalist movement after the outbreak of the war, French control of the ports was seen also as a potentially crucial factor in the future of Franco-Arab relations. Those ports provided ready access to the Hejaz Railway for the very large numbers of Muslim pilgrims on their way to and from Mecca and Medina.[10]

The secret negotiations between McMahon and Hussein, and most especially the former's commitment to support Arab nationalist aims in Syria, made it imperative that Britain reach an understanding with France as soon as possible. Not to do so would leave Britain open to charges of perfidy and could affect the cohesion of the Entente at a time when it was engaged in a hard-fought world war. The French were aware that the British officials in Cairo were talking to the Arabs about Syria, a country of primary French interest in the Middle East, and one which Paris regarded almost as a dependency. The draft agreement between France and Britain regarding a postwar settlement in the

Middle East was negotiated quickly, since both were anxious to come to an agreement rather than have the question linger as a festering sore that might affect the joint war effort. However, it is of interest to note that while the British Foreign Office was quite pleased with the results, the War Office was notably less sanguine about it. William R. Hall, head of intelligence at the Admiralty, had a number of reservations about the draft, one of which concerned the way it dealt with Palestine and the Jews. In essence, the Sykes–Picot Agreement called for the triple partition of Palestine into French, British and internationally administered zones that would also accommodate Arab nationalist demands to some extent. The agreement seemed to be predicated on the assumption that Jewish interest in Palestine was primarily sentimental and would be accommodated by the proposed internationalization of Jerusalem and its environs, while the rest of the country was left to the Arabs under European supervision. Hall, by contrast, had a much better sense of the character of Zionist aspirations in Palestine. He argued that "the Jews have a strong material, and a very strong political, interest in the future of the country." He anticipated significant Jewish opposition "throughout the world, to any scheme recognizing Arab independence and foreshadowing Arab predominance in the southern Near East."[11]

Although the specifics of Sir Mark Sykes's negotiations with Georges Picot that began in November 1915 and were concluded on March 9, 1916, were confidential, it was not long before some intimations of what was going on became known in British Zionist circles. There was mounting suspicion that Foreign Secretary Sir Edward Grey was contemplating a joint declaration by Britain, France and Russia about Zionist aspirations that suggested a possible three-power condominium in Palestine. This generated strongly critical commentaries in the organ of the British Palestine Committee, *Palestine,* that evoked complaints from Sykes to Chaim Weizmann, who had become the principal Zionist leader in England. Sykes suggested that the articles, which were widely circulated, were adversely affecting the conduct of his negotiations. Presumably, it made it appear that Sykes was deliberately leaking the information to the Zionists. In response to Sykes's repeated complaints about the critical commentaries appearing in *Palestine,* Israel Sieff, who was responsible for the publication, wrote to Weizmann on February 4, 1916: "I cannot too strongly insist upon the danger of allowing Sir Mark to believe that we Zionists can agree to a condominium . . . if we do not combat this idea from the outset." Again on February 19 Sieff wrote: "There is no doubt in my mind that Sir M. has come to an agreement with the Arabs and his interest in Jewish political aspirations in Palestine is only secondary. . . . I am sure that you will concede that to us Jews, Palestine without the whole of the Hauran and the Hejaz Railway, means not only a cramped and restricted Palestine without any hope of extension, but also a Palestine continually threatened by a strong Arab group which will make our position East of the Jordan precarious for all time." Sieff then went on to plead with Weizmann not to allow the future of the Jewish state to be stifled before it was even born, nor to amputate important parts of it for the sake of an agreement with the Arabs. While Sykes's negotiations on behalf of the Zionists were appreciated, "it would be very dangerous for us to give way" on the Hauran and Hejaz Railway.[12]

The agreement had indeed divided the Near East into three major zones of control and influence. The Blue Zone, which included Cilicia and the coastal area from Alexandretta south as far as Acre, encompassing Lebanon, the northern Galilee and the Hula region, was to be assigned to France. In addition, a French protectorate was to be established in the interior of Syria north of the Yarmuk River and the Mosul region of Upper Mesopotamia. The Red Zone, which included Central and Lower Mesopotamia (Iraq), was allocated to Britain. A British protectorate was also to be established over the region between the Red Sea and Iraq, south of the Yarmuk, which included the Negev and southern Transjordan. The two protectorates together were to constitute a vaguely conceived single Arab state. The Brown Zone, which included the area of Central Palestine from Acre south to Gaza and east to the Sea of Galilee, the Jordan River and the Dead Sea, was to be a condominium of France, Britain and Russia. The Brown Zone, which was essentially the region surrounding Jerusalem, Nazareth and Bethlehem, was a compromise to accommodate Russian interest in the holy places of importance to the Orthodox Church. While the agreement was in apparent conflict with the vague commitments made to the Arabs through the Hussein-McMahon correspondence, as well as with the commitments that were soon to be made to the Zionists, all the documentation involved was considered to be sufficiently vague as to allow it to be construed in any manner that would best serve British interests once the fighting ended. And, in fact, by the time the ink was dry on the Sykes-Picot Agreement, a series of events had taken place which made it no longer palatable to the British, especially with regard to Palestine.

Almost immediately after the agreement was concluded, the Russians decided that they would be willing to see the Brown Zone transferred to the French Blue Zone in exchange for territorial concessions in Turkish Armenia. They attached two stipulations. One was that the Orthodox holy places be internationalized and allowed unimpeded access to the sea. The second was that France obtain Britain's consent to the change. The British, however, were opposed to the idea and became concerned about Franco-Russian collusion in Palestine that might be detrimental to Britain's interests. This led Lord Crewe, acting on behalf of Foreign Secretary Grey, to seek ways of strengthening Britain's hand in Palestine. One way was through the support of Zionist settlement there. The argument was that if the British took the lead in sponsoring Jewish settlement in Palestine, the settlers themselves would insist on the retention of British political influence there and would have the support in this of the Jews of the world, including those of the other Entente countries. Accordingly, on March 11, 1916, Grey (Crewe) sent a message to the Allied governments, through the British ambassadors in Paris and Petrograd, which spoke of the benefits to be realized in terms of Jewish support for the war effort from the United States, if the allied governments would endorse an arrangement supportive of Jewish colonization in Palestine. The cable went on to say: "We consider, however, that the scheme might be made far more attractive to the majority of Jews if it held out to them the prospect that when in course of time the Jewish colonists in Palestine grow strong enough to cope with the Arab population they may be allowed to take the management of the internal affairs of Palestine (with the exception of Jerusalem and the Holy Places) into their own hands." It then noted, reflecting the wave of criticism the Foreign Office had received from the Zionists in England, "that some influential Zionist opinion would be opposed to an international protectorate." Surprisingly, the Russian minister Sazonov responded that the Russian government viewed the "proposed settlement of Jews in Palestine with sympathy, but that the Holy Places must be excluded from any such scheme." The French, on the other hand, responded rather negatively, as the Foreign Office had expected.[13]

Another consideration of importance was the dramatic change in the British perception of the strategic importance of Palestine as the war progressed. The primary British strategic concern in the region was the protection of the Suez Canal and the waterways leading to India. Before the war, it was generally assumed that a substantial desert region such as Sinai was the equivalent of a fortified frontier. Since the Egyptian-Turkish boundary was set across the eastern end of the Sinai Desert, the latter served as a natural barrier of sufficient depth to provide adequate protection against a land assault on the Suez Canal. However, in 1915, a substantial and well-equipped Turkish force had crossed the desert and penetrated as far as the canal. Then, a year later, a British force crossed the Sinai from Egypt, laying a railroad and pipeline as it advanced. It then seized El Arish and was poised to attack Gaza. It was now evident that advances in military technology had increased mobility to the point where the Sinai Desert itself could no longer be considered as an adequate defensive barrier. It therefore became important to assure that Palestine itself was in friendly hands in order to ensure the security of the canal. The Sykes-Picot Agreement, however, assigned Syria to France; and France had made it clear that it considered Syria to include central Palestine, notwithstanding its designation as the international Brown Zone. Furthermore, the agreement explicitly required that all prewar concessions in Palestine granted by the Turks were to be recognized as valid and ongoing after the war. This meant that the French railway concessions there would be developed further, thereby challenging Britain's own plans for the future of the region.

Another factor of some importance affecting British perceptions of the Middle East during this period was its rather unrealistic estimate of the extent to which the Jews of Turkey were able to influence Ottoman policy, as well as the assumed ramifications of this on the attitude of Jews elsewhere toward support of the war aims of the Entente Powers, especially in the United States. The British perception was based to some degree on the prewar view (August 22, 1910) of the British Embassy in Constantinople that the ruling Committee of Union and Progress represented "a Judaeo-Turkish dual alliance, the Turks supplying a splendid military material and the Jews the brain, enterprise, money . . . and a strong press influence in Europe. . . . The Jews, in order to maintain their position of influence in Young Turkey circles, have to play up to, if not encourage, Turkish "nationalistic" tendencies, and the two elements make a distinctive strong combination."[14] With the outbreak of the war, and the alignment of Turkey with Germany, the Foreign Office began to discuss whether there were any practicable ways of severing the Turco-Jewish alliance in order to weaken Turkey's ability to continue to prosecute the war. A good example of this internal debate is the minute prepared by Hugh O'Beirne on February 28, 1916: "It has been suggested to me that if we could offer the Jews an arrangement as to Palestine which would strongly appeal to them we might conceivably be able to strike a bargain with them as to withdrawing their support from the Young Turk Government which would then automatically collapse."[15]

Notwithstanding the ongoing discussion of the question in British government circles, nothing of any significance happened until after the Lloyd George government took power in December 1916. By contrast with the predecessor Asquith administration, which was traditionally Europe-oriented, David Lloyd George was an "Easterner"; that is, he was focused on the needs of the empire in Africa and Asia. It quickly became clear that none of the arrangements for the region between Syria and Egypt that had previously been worked out were any longer considered acceptable. In particular, Britain was now adamantly opposed to the internationalization of Palestine. This policy change had the complete support of the Zionist Organization, which had long agitated against the truncation of Palestine. Furthermore, since neither the Sykes-Picot Agreement nor McMahon's promises to Hussein were solemnized by a formal treaty, the Lloyd George government did not feel irrevocably bound by them. In April

1917, an interdepartmental Sub-Committee on Territorial Desiderata was established under the chairmanship of Lord Curzon. The basic assumption of the committee was that there would be no decisive victory in the war. Instead, it was expected to end in an armistice followed by a negotiated settlement favorable to the Entente. Because of this, it was seen as essential to take the steps necessary with respect to both Germany and Turkey to ensure that neither belligerent would be in a position once again in the foreseeable future to reopen hostilities with Britain. As one guideline for policy, the committee recommended the adoption of the principle that British policy must seek "to eliminate all bases, actual or potential, which might be used by Germany to threaten the sea communications of the British Empire, or which might constitute a direct military or political menace to any of its constituent parts."[16]

General Jan Smuts, who was a leading member of the committee, took a special interest in Palestine and argued that the security of communications between Egypt and the East could only be assured if the country, along with Mesopotamia, came under British control. The committee accepted Smuts's arguments and included the following in its recommendations to the Cabinet:

> The acquisition by Germany—through her control of Turkey—of political and military control in Palestine and Mesopotamia would imperil communication between the United Kingdom, on the one hand, and the East and Australasia, on the other, through the Suez Canal, and would directly threaten the security of Egypt and India. It is of great importance that both Palestine and Mesopotamia should be under British control. To ensure this it is desirable that His Majesty's Government should secure such modification of the Agreement with France of May 1916 as would give Great Britain definite and exclusive control over Palestine and would take the frontier of the British sphere of control to the river Leontes and North of the Hauran. Turkish rule should never be restored in Palestine or Mesopotamia.[17]

The prime minister, even before receiving the committee's recommendation, had already raised the question of Palestine coming under British control at the Inter-Allied Conference at St. Jean de Maurienne in April 1917. However, it was received rather coolly by the other Entente members. Indeed, the conference had concluded that both French and Italian forces should participate in the Palestine campaign, a decision that was greeted in the Italian press as a prelude to the establishment of an international regime over the holy places as called for in the Sykes-Picot Agreement.[18] The requirements of British policy were now clear. It remained to find a way to undo the specific constraints of the Sykes-Picot Agreement with regard to Palestine.

Thus it came about at the beginning of 1917 that Sir Mark Sykes, coauthor of the Sykes-Picot Agreement, began secret exploratory meetings with the Zionist leaders in Britain to determine whether the latter might be helpful in effectively nullifying the agreement that bore his name. There is a general presumption that the contacts were kept secret not so much to keep the French from finding out about them as to keep the British Foreign Office itself in the dark. This was necessary from Sykes's standpoint in order to avoid interference from the regular Foreign Office bureaucrats, who were expected to oppose on principle any tampering with the international agreement. Sykes was determined to find a way to avoid a direct confrontation with France over Palestine that might necessitate an overt British repudiation of the agreement.

On February 7, 1917, Sykes met with a number of prominent Zionist leaders who were as yet unaware of the details of the agreement with the French. Disingenuously, he told them that "no pledge had been given by the British government to France with regard to Palestine and the question has been kept open" in the negotiations regarding the postwar settlement in the Near East.[19] He suggested that the French, who really had no standing to make any claims on Palestine, were likely to be the most troublesome opponents of Zionist aspirations. He indicated that he had already convinced even the Russian foreign minister, S. D. Sazonov, to support Zionist colonization. The French thus remained the major stumbling block to complete agreement on the matter among the Entente Powers. It would therefore be in the Zionist interest, he argued, to help Britain find a way to get the French to back down from their claims, which would result in the attachment of Palestine to Lebanon and Syria. In effect, Sykes's scheme was that the Zionists should spearhead the demand that Palestine come under British control in exchange for a commitment that the Zionists would be accorded a privileged position to pursue their goals there under British sponsorship. One means of achieving these goals would be through the establishment of a Zionist chartered company, having limited autonomy, that would organize and oversee the colonization and settlement program. Bearing in mind the agreed southern limits of the Blue Zone assigned to the French, Sykes proposed that the chartered company limit its colonization activity to a region whose northern boundary would be a line drawn from Acre to the east of the Jordan. The southern limit, which would abut British-controlled territory north of the Sinai, could be negotiated later with the British government. Also bearing in mind French and Russian sensibilities with regard to the holy sites of Christendom, he proposed that the area along the railroad between Jerusalem and Jaffa be internationalized.

The Zionist leaders took strong exception to these proposals since the latter appeared to disregard the existing realities of Zionist settlement in Palestine. They noted that the northern limit of settlement proposed by Sykes would exclude the already existing Jewish colonies in the Upper Galilee, and would place them under French jurisdiction. Furthermore, the proposed international zone would exclude Jerusalem and the existing Jewish settlements near Jaffa from the Jewish homeland. Such a severely delimited zone of settlement was not what the Zionists had in mind, nor was it one that they were prepared to accept. Sykes, bearing in mind the limits to how far he might dare push the French, suggested in response that, notwithstanding the Zionists' concerns and reservations, such arrangements might be required to accommodate the French, who were showing little interest in the Zionist enterprise.[20]

It seems quite clear, in retrospect, that Sykes really had a very weak grasp of what Zionism was all about. One consequence of this deficiency was his readiness to concoct abstract schemes for resolving the conflicting interests of the various claimants to the territory of Palestine. At one point, during his negotiations with Picot in March 1917, he proposed, presumably in reflection of his continuing belief in the importance of the Arabs to the war effort and the need to accommodate their ambitions, that one of Hussein's sons be designated as sultan of Palestine, with Britain and France serving as guarantors of the independent state. A Zionist chartered company, presumably having some sort of extraterritorial status, would be provided for in the constitution of the state, and the Jewish colonists would become full citizens of the Arab state. At the same time, Britain would undertake to arbitrate any disputes between the Palestine government and the company. This complex, unworkable and rather naive scheme was predicated on the assumption that since the Zionists were not publicly seeking a government in Palestine, but only the right of colonization in a Jewish homeland, they would be willing to agree to limited autonomy under Arab sovereignty. After all, the existing settlements in the country had long been under Turkish rule. Why would the Zionists not agree to their continuation and expansion under Arab rule, as long as they had a British guarantee for their chartered company? This scheme was dismissed out of hand as unrealistic at the Foreign Office. Harold Nicolson pointed out: "It is clear that the Chartered Jewish Company, suggested by Sir M. Sykes, would very soon gain complete administrative, financial and executive authority in the new State, but our real object in raising the question is to find something with which to dazzle Jewish opinion—and I much doubt whether an Arab Sultanate would have that effect."[21] Notwithstanding the negative reaction to his plan in the Foreign Office, Sykes communicated it to the Zionist leaders in London through Herbert Samuel.

On April 8, Sykes wrote to the foreign secretary, Lord Balfour, apprising him of the plan to use the Zionists as an instrument for keeping the French out of Palestine. He noted that at the moment it might be "dangerous to moot the idea of a British Palestine, but if the French agree to recognize Jewish Nationalism and all that it carries with it as a Palestinian political factor, I think it will prove a step in the right direction, and will tend to pave the way to Great Britain being appointed patron of Palestine."[22]

Reflecting their concerns over Sykes's apparent readiness to negotiate away their interests, the Zionist leadership mounted a concerted campaign in France, Italy, Russia, the United States and, perhaps most especially, in Britain to gain public recognition and approbation of Zionist aspirations. This campaign soon began to have positive results, most importantly in France. In the meantime, the overthrow of the Russian tsar in March 1917 occasioned a renewed urgency to British efforts to draw the Zionists closer. There was a strong concern that without the tsar, Russia's contribution to the war effort might come to an end, bringing a collapse of the eastern front. It was considered imperative that everything possible be done to keep the new provisional government committed to continuing in the war, and the Zionists were seen as an instrument that might help in achieving that goal. It was believed that the Jews of Western Europe and the United States could have significant influence on their coreligionists in Russia, many of whom were in the forefront of the socialist forces asserting themselves there. This had the effect of opening many doors in London, presenting new opportunities for the Zionist leaders to assert the Zionist cause.

The Zionist leadership had been aware for more than a year of the existence of a secret Anglo-French agreement on Palestine. However, it was not until the middle of April 1917 that Chaim Weizmann first became formally aware of the existence of the Sykes-Picot Agreement and its provisions. On April 25, he met with Lord Robert Cecil at the Foreign Office and expressed his concern

> that this arrangement embodies all the faults of an Anglo-French and an international settlement and is, moreover, aggravated by the fact that Palestine is cut up in two halves and the Jewish colonizing effort, which had been going on before the war for more than thirty years, is thus annihilated. By the separation of Galilee from Judea, Palestine has been deprived of a very valuable part of the country. . . . The Zionists will particularly suffer because around the Lake of Tiberias the country is dotted with Jewish colonies. . . . We would always consider it an unjust partition and it would certainly constitute a Jewish *irredenta*.[23]

Throughout 1917, the Zionist Organization, through its publication, *Palestine*, kept up a barrage of critical commentary on the question of the boundaries of Palestine. Laying aside the maximalist claims of Orthodox Jews to Palestine in its biblical dimensions, the secular leadership of the Jewish national movement based their claims on geopolitical and security grounds. Security for the Jewish national homeland would require control over the desert areas to the south and east, from which repeated nomadic invasions of Palestine had taken place in the past. In the north, similar considerations would require control of the Bekaa Valley between the Lebanon and Mount Hermon, the historic gateway into the country from Syria. Furthermore, northern Palestine had repeatedly been severed from the center and south by armies sweeping into the Jezreel Valley from the Hauran and the Yarmuk Valley. It was thus essential that these territories be included within the homeland to maintain its integrity. From the standpoint of economic viability, the country would have to develop both its industrial and agricultural bases to make it capable of absorbing the immigration necessary to meeting the Zionist aims. Since the country was almost completely lacking in coal or petroleum, and had very little water resources, it was essential that the falls of the Litani and Yarmuk rivers be included within its boundaries to assure a constant supply of adequate hydroelectric power. In addition, the only remaining timber stands in the region were in the Gilead, in Transjordania. Finally, since the only remaining large continuous stretches of arable land were to be found in the Negev and Transjordania, these territories were essential to Palestine's economic viability as well. The British government was thus well aware that the Zionists in London had done their homework, and that the arbitrary lines drawn on the Sykes-Picot map would be fought against vigorously and relentlessly by the proponents of the Zionist cause.

By late spring, having overcome some significant intracommunal problems that inhibited their freedom of action, the Zionists in London were now more able to press their demands for a formal public commitment from the British government. On June 13, Weizmann wrote to Sir Ronald Graham, assistant undersecretary at the Foreign Office, that "it appears desirable from every point of view that the British Government should give expression to its sympathy and support of the Zionist claims on Palestine. In fact, it need only confirm the view which eminent and representative members of the Government have many times expressed to us, and which have formed the basis of our negotiations throughout the long period of almost three years."[24] The Foreign Office evidently agreed and, at the suggestion of Lord

Balfour, the foreign secretary, the Zionists were invited to submit a draft statement for consideration. After much internal debate among the Zionist leadership and many drafts, it was decided to sacrifice comprehensiveness to a focus on fundamental principles. Accordingly, on July 18, a draft declaration was submitted to Balfour for the approval of the War Cabinet and ultimately for promulgation by the British government. The declaration reduced the broad range of Zionist concerns to two major points:

1. His Majesty's Government accepts the principle that Palestine should be reconstituted as the National Home of the Jewish People.
2. His Majesty's Government will use its best endeavors to secure the achievement of this object and will discuss the necessary methods and means with the Zionist Organization.[25]

The draft declaration came before the War Cabinet for consideration on September 3. The British leaders were now confronted by a seemingly intractable dilemma. On the one hand, they continued to see the value of an alliance with the Zionists in terms of their aims for a British Palestine. On the other hand, what the Zionists were asking of them implied long-term commitments that they might not be able or even wish to fulfill, given the prevailing understandings among the Entente Powers regarding the postwar settlement. Since they were unable to reach a firm decision on the matter, the question of the draft declaration was simply allowed to lapse from the Cabinet's agenda. Furthermore, and probably of far greater importance than the Cabinet's concern about the Allies, there was the staunch opposition to the Zionist declaration by the ardently anti-Zionist Jewish member of the War Cabinet, Sir Edwin Montagu. In the meantime, Graham at the Foreign Office was becoming increasingly concerned over the delay in getting the Cabinet to take action and its possible negative consequences. He wrote: "The result of this delay is that the Zionist leaders are rendered uncertain, if not dissatisfied, and that their propaganda on behalf of the Allies has practically ceased. . . . We are anxious to induce M. Sokolow to proceed to Russia as soon as possible with a view to impressing the British case upon the Jews and to arousing Jewish enthusiasm for the expulsion of the Turks from Palestine . . . but he will not go until this question of an assurance is settled nor will Dr Weizmann take any more active steps."[26]

That same day, Graham also prepared a minute for the record that further stressed the potential seriousness of continued delay by the Cabinet:

> This further delay will have a deplorable result and may jeopardize the whole Jewish situation. At the present moment uncertainty as regards the attitude of His Majesty's Government on this question is growing into suspicion and not only are we losing the very valuable co-operation of the Zionist forces in Russia and America, but we may bring them into antagonism with us and throw the Zionists into the arms of the Germans, who would only be too ready to welcome this opportunity. . . .
>
> We might at any moment be confronted by a German move on the Zionist question and it must be remembered that Zionism was originally if not a German at any rate an Austrian idea. The French have already given an assurance of sympathy to the Zionists on the same lines as is now proposed for His Majesty's Government, though in rather more definite terms. The Italian Government and the Vatican have expressed their sympathy and we know that President Wilson is sympathetic and is prepared to make a declaration at the proper moment. . . .
>
> The moment this assurance is granted, the Zionist Jews are prepared to start an active pro-Allied propaganda throughout the world. . . . I earnestly trust that unless there is a very good reason to the contrary the assurance from His Majesty's Government should be given at once.[27]

Graham's concerns were further reflected in Balfour's statement to the War Cabinet on October 4, in which he cautioned that continued delay on the question would play into Germany's hands. Under Balfour's pressure, Montagu's parochial objections were ultimately overridden. When Herbert Samuel was solicited for his views on the draft declaration, he responded that the policy embodied therein "seems to me to be right. If the Turks are left ostensibly in control of Palestine, the country is likely to fall in course of time under German influence. If Germany or any other Continental Power is dominant there, Egypt would be exposed to constant menace. The best safeguard would be the establishment of a large Jewish population, preferably under British protection."[28]

The question of the boundaries within which the Jewish National Home was to be construed was also an item of some discussion. Lord Curzon had submitted a memorandum on the issue to the Cabinet in which he suggested that the proposed declaration should apply to a region of approximately 10,000 square miles, "including 4,000 square miles to the east of the Jordan."[29] After some further careful redrafting at the Foreign Office, the declaration was approved by the War Cabinet on October 31, and tramsitted in the form of a letter to Lord Rothschild on November 2. It stated: "His Majesty's Government view with favour the establishment in Palestine of a national home for the Jewish people, and will use their best endeavors to facilitate the achievement of this object, it being clearly understood that nothing shall be done which may prejudice the civil and religious rights of existing non-Jewish communities in Palestine, or the rights and political status enjoyed by Jews in any other country."[30]

Notwithstanding the purposeful ambiguity of phrases such as "*a* national home" and "use their best endeavors," the declaration was received almost universally as the initial step toward the creation of a Jewish state in Palestine. As far as most realistic observers were concerned, the "national home" of the Balfour Declaration was the same as the "home" of the Zionist Basel Resolution of 1897. "Home" was a euphemism for a future state. That this was clearly understood was demonstrated by David Lloyd George's description of the intentions of the War Cabinet in approving the declaration:

> It was not their idea that a Jewish State should be set up immediately by the Peace Treaty without reference to the wishes of the majority of the inhabitants. On the other hand, it was contemplated that when the time arrived for according representative institutions in Palestine, if the Jews had meanwhile responded to the opportunity afforded them by the idea of a National Home and had become a definite majority of the inhabitants, then Palestine would thus become a Jewish Commonwealth.[31]

The key word here is "immediately." There was no question in their minds that the declaration contemplated an eventual Jewish state.

The Anglo-Zionist Conspiracy

At the time of the Balfour Declaration, as Graham had warned, the German government was doing whatever it could to bring the Zionist movement to its support in the hope that this might help undermine the Allied war effort. In conjunction with Turkey, it was even developing a plan for a chartered company for Zionists that would have local autonomy and a right of immigration into Palestine.[32] There is thus a certain irony in the fact that the much dreaded German declaration of support for Zionist aspirations was finally issued on January 5, 1918, two months too late to have any impact. The German under-secretary of state, Freiherr Axel von dem Bussche-Haddenhausen, stated:

> With regard to the aspirations of Jewry, especially of the Zionists, towards Palestine, we welcome the recent statement of Talaat Pasha, the Grand Vizier, as well as the intentions of the Ottoman Government, made in accordance with its traditional friendship towards the Jews in general, to promote a flourishing Jewish settlement in Palestine, in particular by means of unrestricted immigration and settlement within the absorptive capacity of the country; local self-government in accordance with the country's laws, and the free development of their civilization.[33]

The intense British concern over what the Germans might do with regard to the Zionists pointedly suggests that the pronouncement of British support for Zionism, as reflected in the Balfour Declaration, had fundamentally very little to do with the effectiveness of Zionist propaganda in Britain or the pro-Zionist sympathies of certain British officials. It was essentially nothing more than a wartime measure taken by the British government exclusively for the furtherance of tangible British national and imperial objectives. The primary aim was not to give the Jews the basis for a state in Palestine any more than the McMahon correspondence was intended to lay the basis for a pan-Arab state stretching from the Arabian Sea to the Turkish border. Indeed, both were steps taken to help make the victory over Germany and Turkey more definitive and to assure that Britain's strategic interests in the Near East would be well served. At the time that the War Cabinet finally decided to take action on the question, it was already clear that the Zionists were probably no longer needed to help reverse the provisions of the Sykes-Picot Agreement that dealt with Palestine. Because of Britain's overwhelming commitment of forces to the region, it was generally expected, even by the French, that London would have the final say regarding the disposition of Turkish territories in the Near East. There were, however, other compelling reasons for the continued courtship of the Zionists. The Russian Revolution seemed to be heading in the direction of a separate peace with Germany, and Britain wanted to do whatever it could to prevent or delay the collapse of the eastern front. Furthermore, it was believed that the Zionists could be helpful in overcoming the reluctance of many in the United States who were not enthusiastic about American involvement in a European war. Thus, from the perspective of British policy makers, both Weizmann and the Zionists and Hussein and the Arab nationalists provided fortuitous opportunities to advance British aims at very little cost.

Once the Balfour Declaration had been issued, it became politically possible for a Jewish Legion to be formed within the British army. Vladimir Jabotinsky had worked for this indefatigably since 1916. The legion, under the command of Colonel John H. Patterson, who had previously commanded the Zion Mule Corps, arrived in Egypt at the end of February 1918. It soon distinguished itself in battle in Palestine. The legion, some six thousand volunteers, played a significant role in the final campaign to drive the Turks out of the country. Successfully carrying out its responsibility for capturing and holding the strongly defended Umm es Shert ford across the Jordan, the legion allowed the British cavalry to sweep across the river where, after a ten-day battle, they destroyed the Turkish Fourth Army, winning the battle for Palestine.[34]

An agreement was also reached between the Zionist Organization and the British government to establish a Zionist Commission, under Weizmann's leadership, that would go to Palestine to begin to lay the foundations for the forthcoming Jewish National Home. On March 2, 1918, Balfour informed the chief political officer in Palestine, General Gilbert Clayton, about the functions and status of the Zionist Commission which was on its way to the country. He told Clayton that the commission was being sent by the government "in order to assist you in carrying into effect such measures as can be taken, consistent with your operations, to give concrete form to this Declaration."[35]

Clayton reported to Balfour some six weeks later on his views about the commission's aims and the problems faced by the British administration in Palestine in promoting them. On April 18, he wrote that it was inevitable that the British officials "should experience some difficulties in consequence of the fact that up to date our policy has been directed towards securing Arab sympathy in view of our Arab commitments. It is not easy therefore to switch over to Zionism all at once in the face of a considerable degree of Arab distrust and suspicion." Furthermore, he suggested, "in the interest of Zionism itself, it is very necessary to proceed with caution." He indicated that he had explained this to Weizmann so that the latter might better appreciate why the military administration found it necessary "to turn down, or delay, some of the schemes put forward by the Commission. . . . Arab opinion both in Palestine and elsewhere is in no condition to support an overdose of Zionism just now." Clayton concluded his report with an urgent request that the government allow the local officials to deal with the Zionist Commission according to their best judgment and not to force them "into precipitate action which might well wreck our whole policy, both Arab and Zionist."[36] This report reflected Clayton's considered judgment that Zionist aims were in direct conflict with Arab aims and were essentially irreconcilable. However, his views were not necessarily reflective of those of all the British experts in the region.

Two days after Clayton issued his report to Balfour, Major Kinnahan Cornwallis, director of the Arab Bureau in Cairo, sent a confidential report to his superior on the state of Arab opinion regarding the Zionist Commission. He flatly contradicted Clayton's assertion that the military administration in Palestine was fully informed on the Zionist program and the commitments of the British government in such regard. He noted that, since the arrival of the commission, "the Palestinians tend more and more to divorce themselves from Syria and most of the criticisms are now coming from Syrians, who having no direct interest in the matter, seek to disguise the fact by an exaggerated expression of concern."[37] A similar, more positive assessment was sent by

Captain Ormsby-Gore, liaison officer with the commission, to the head of the Cabinet Secretariat on April 19. It was thus clear that there was a sharp divergence of view among the British experts regarding the impact of and reaction to the Zionist enterprise. It was the perspective of Clayton, however, whether well founded or not, that dominated the attitude of the British administration in Palestine, and later in London as well. Symptomatic of this perspective was the fact that the British administration did not permit the formal publication of the Balfour Declaration in Palestine until after the San Remo Conference in 1920. In view of this, the highly problematic relations between the Zionists and the British that characterized the next thirty years are not at all surprising.

3

The Period of Hashemite-Zionist Cooperation

With the signing of the armistice on October 30, 1918, the British were unquestionably in a dominant position in the Middle East. British forces in the region numbered some 200,000 whereas the French had a force of only some 6,000. As Lloyd George had intended from the moment he took over as prime minister in 1916, it was now time to do away with some of the more unacceptable terms of the Sykes-Picot Agreement. The time was propitious since the French prime minister, Georges Clemenceau, was far more interested in the politics of and the French position in Europe than in the Middle East. He was primarily concerned about obtaining French control of the Rhine and the Saar basin, and he needed British backing for his plans. Lloyd George, however, was disinclined to support French aims along the German frontier because it was not in Britain's interest to alter the balance of power in Europe in a way that would lead to French supremacy. It was clear to Clemenceau that if he wished to obtain Lloyd George's support he would have to pay a substantial price. He came to London in November 1918 to determine just what that price was. As Lloyd George was to note later, "When Clemenceau came to London after the War, I drove with him to the French Embassy through cheering crowds. After we reached the Embassy he asked me what it was I specifically wanted from the French. I instantly replied that I wanted Mosul attached to Irak, and Palestine from Dan to Beersheba under British control. Without any hesitation he agreed."[1] What Clemenceau actually agreed to was an exchange of a clear claim to Mosul and Palestine for British support of French claims on the Rhine plus a share of the oil from Mosul, a guarantee of unconditional British support at the peace conference on the basis of the previously negotiated secret agreements and, once the mandates system was established, support for France's receipt of the mandate over Syria.[2]

It was quite clear by early 1918 that the contradictory promises made to both the Arabs and the Jews with regard to Palestine, and particularly those portions to the east of the Jordan such as the Hauran, necessitated that the leaders of both client groups reach a mutual understanding. Consequently, on June 4, under British auspices, Weizmann went to see Feisal at his headquarters at Wadi Wahaida, near Aqaba in Transjordan. In describing the occasion in a letter to his wife dated June 17, Weizmann wrote: ". . . I made the acquaintance of Feisal, son of the King of the Hedjaz. . . . He is not interested in Palestine, but on the other hand he wants Damascus and the whole of northern Syria. He talked with great animosity against the French, who want to get their hands on Syria. He expects a great deal from collaboration with the Jews! He is contemptuous of the Palestinian Arabs whom he doesn't even regard as Arabs."[3]

Weizmann later amplified on the substance of the discussion:

> After the usual exchange of politenesses, I explained to him the mission on which I had come to Palestine, our desire to do everything in our power to allay Arab fears and susceptibilities, and our hope that he would lend us his powerful moral support. He asked me a great many questions about the Zionist program, and I found him by no means uninformed. At this time, it must be remembered, Palestine and Trans-Jordan were one and the same thing, and I stressed the fact that there was a great deal of room in the country if intensive development were applied, and that the lot of the Arabs would be greatly improved through our work there. With all this I found the Emir in full agreement, as Lawrence later confirmed to me by letter.[4]

Brigadier Gilbert F. Clayton, the British political officer who orchestrated the Weizmann-Feisal relationship, held separate conversations with both Feisal and Weizmann subsequent to their desert meeting, and reported to the foreign secretary as follows:

> Sherif Faisal sees in Zionism a force which, if enlisted on his side, may furnish him with the necessary economic support, but which bears what may be described as an "un-national" complexion. With the help of Zionism, he thinks he may counter international concessionaires . . . , French political influence exerted through clericals and financiers, and all these forces which tend towards foreign exploitation and which are detrimental to development on national lines. As regards political support, he recognises in Zionism an "international" influence which permeates every country from which the future Syrian State may have anything to hope or fear. Finally, behind Zionism and working through it, he reckons on the British Empire on which in the last resort he places his trust. . . .
> Dr. Weizmann realises that the development of those ideals which lie behind Zionism depends upon the establishment in Palestine of a centre of Jewish culture and sentiment, based on the soil itself, to which all Jewry will turn and which will justify its political existence by providing a bridge between East and West. An essential factor to the realisation of this ideal is that the future Jewish Palestine should be linked in close sympathy with the States by which it is surrounded. This is a condition of its development, and, indeed, of its existence.[5]

Clayton also reported the views of Colonel Pierre C. Joyce, who was also present at the meeting and gave "as his private opinion that Feisal really welcomed Jewish cooperation and considered it essential to future Arab ambitions though unable to express any very definite views in absence of his father. . . . Feisal fully realizes the future possibility of a Jewish Palestine and would probably accept it if it assisted Arab expansion further north."[6] In Joyce's own record of the meeting, he noted that "Dr. Weizmann pointed out that the Jews do not propose setting up a Jewish Government but would like to work under British protection with a view to colonising the country without in any way encroaching on anybody's legitimate interests." Feisal, he noted, personally "accepted the possibility of future Jewish claims to territory in Palestine."⁷ It seemed clear, however, given that Feisal was supposedly acting on behalf of his father, that a true cementing of Zionist-Hashemite relations required a meeting between Weizmann and Hussein. But such a meeting was adamantly opposed by D. G. Hogarth of the Arab Bureau. In an undated secret note written from the Hejaz in August or September 1918, Hogarth observed that "Dr. Weizmann hopes for a completely Jewish Palestine in fifty years, and a Jewish Palestine under a British facade for the moment. He is fighting for his own lead among British and American Jews: if he can offer these the spectacle of British help and Arab willingness to allow Jewish enterprise free scope in all their provinces and in Syria, he will then secure the financial backing that will make Judea a reality."⁸ It was Hogarth's view that a Weizmann-Hussein meeting was premature since neither was really in a position to undertake such a series of commitments at the time. The encounter never took place.

After the collapse of the Turkish front in October 1918, the British commander General Allenby established three Occupied Enemy Territory Administrations (OETA's) that covered the zones of the Sykes-Picot Agreement. OETA North included the Blue Zone assigned to the French, that is, the Syrian and Lebanese coasts. OETA South covered the Brown Zone (Palestine west of the Jordan), and OETA East encompassed the combined areas demarcated in the Sykes-Picot Agreement for French and British protectorates into a single administrative area which they turned over to Feisal for the establishment of a civil regime. As soon as these administrative divisions became known, strong protests emerged from the Zionist community over the arbitrary separation of Transjordan from Cisjordan, which were both considered to be equally integral parts of Palestine. Herbert Samuel promptly attempted to reassure the Zionist public that "there shall be no division of Palestine . . . the ancient, historic and natural boundaries of the land shall be respected"; and Lord Bryce stated, "You cannot separate Eastern from Western Palestine."⁹

In the meantime, Feisal was anxiously attempting to establish his regime in Damascus but was plagued by a crippling dearth of resources. He discreetly sought, presumably on the basis of his

Hashemite-Zionist Cooperation

June meeting with Weizmann, financial support from Zionist sources. On October 27, David Eder telegraphed Weizmann from Palestine to inform him of Feisal's grave financial situation. Given Feisal's demonstration of interest in a loan and financial advice from the Zionists, Eder suggested that it was the appropriate moment to enter into serious negotiations with him.[10] Weizmann, however, was concerned about the possible negative longer-range implications of such a move and proposed to wait. On November 5, he wrote to Clayton (who had transmitted Eder's message to London and was probably Feisal's contact in the matter) that the idea had been given thorough consideration, and

> We came to the following conclusion: that it is not desirable at present to advance any money to Feysal, as it may seriously prejudice our good relations. If we lend money to Feysal at present, we lay ourselves open to a reproach that we are attempting to put him and his friends under an obligation. . . .
>
> I have pointed out to my fellow-Zionists that the fundamental principle on which co-operation with Feysal must be established is that whatever we do there must be done in the same spirit and under the same conditions as we do things for ourselves. On no account must an impression go abroad that the Jews, whether they are Zionists or non-Zionists, are trying to hunt for concessions in Damascus and are making use of Feysal's financial embarrassment in order to lay their hands on the newly created Arab commonwealth. Nothing would be more disastrous than that, and that is why we have to be so particularly careful now in our negotiations with Feysal.[11]

Feisal and Weizmann met again in London on December 11, 1918. On that occasion, Weizmann took the opportunity to outline the Zionist claims once again in considerable detail. In describing the meeting in a letter of December 16 to Sir Eyre Crowe, he wrote that Feisal had with him a map showing the lines drawn by the Sykes-Picot Agreement and was very upset and indignant about what Britain and France had concocted in their secret negotiations. Feisal then ventured the opinion that if the Sykes-Picot Agreement were actually implemented, it would have fatal consequences for the aspirations of both the Arabs and the Jews. The emir also lamented the weakness of the Arab government in

Damascus as well as its deplorable financial state. With regard to the anti-Jewish disorders that were taking place in Palestine at the time, Weizmann wrote of Feisal,

> He thought that the trouble in Palestine at the present time was fomented by Turkish and pro-Turkish propaganda. The Turks always ruled by trying to divide the races under their sway. The Arabs in Palestine are still used to the methods of Turkish propaganda, but he was quite sure that he and his followers would be able to explain to the Arabs that the advent of the Jews into Palestine was for the good of the country, and that the legitimate interests of the Arab peasants would in no way be interfered with. . . . He assured us on his word of honour that he would do everything to support Jewish demands, and would declare at the Peace Conference that Zionism and the Arab movement were fellow movements, and that complete harmony prevailed between them.[12]

Weizmann also reported on the meeting the following day to the Zionist Commission in Palestine by telegram: "The following not for publication . . . Weizmann had most successful interview with Feisal who found himself in complete agreement with our proposals. He was sure that he would be able to explain to Arabs the advantages to country and thus to themselves of a Jewish Palestine. He assured Weizmann that he would not spare any effort to support Jewish demands at Peace Conference where he would declare that Zionism and Arab movement were fellow-movements and complete harmony prevailed between them."[13] In light of Weizmann's optimistic assessment of his relations with Feisal, it is interesting to note that, at almost the same moment, on December 16, William Yale, the American special intelligence agent in the region, reported that after the Weizmann-Feisal meeting in June, the emir had hired paid agents to stir up sentiment against both the British and the Zionists and to generate public enthusiasm for the Sherifian party and an independent Arab empire under the Hashemites.[14]

Feisal nonetheless gave the Zionists good reason for believing that they had really resolved the problem of Arab-Jewish relations regarding Palestine. In the period immediately before the peace conference in Paris, Feisal had given such indications explicitly and publicly on a number of occasions. In an interview with a Reuters correspondent, published in the London *Times* on

December 12, 1918, Feisal stated: "The two main branches of the Semitic family, Arabs and Jews, understand one another, and I hope that as a result of interchange of ideas at the Peace Conference, which will be guided by ideals of self-determination and nationality, each nation will make definite progress towards the realization of its aspirations. Arabs are not jealous of Zionist Jews, and intend to give them fair play; and the Zionist Jews have assured the Nationalist Arabs of their intention to see that they too have fair play in their respective areas." Once again, at a banquet in his honor given by Lord Rothschild on December 21, Feisal remarked: "No true Arab can be suspicious or afraid of Jewish nationalism. . . . We are demanding Arab freedom, and we should show ourselves unworthy of it, if we did not now, as I do, say to the Jews—welcome back home—and cooperate with them to the limit of the Arab State."[15] On December 27, at a meeting with Edwin Montagu, the secretary of state for India, Feisal stated, in response to a question about Palestine,

> The Arabs were under deep obligations to Great Britain, and that it would ill become them to make difficulties over a question, of which they regard the British Government as the best judges. The Arabs recognise that many conflicting interests are centred in Palestine. They admit the moral claims of the Zionists. They regard the Jews as kinsmen whose just claims they will be glad to see satisfied. They feel that the interests of the Arab inhabitants may safely be left in the hands of the British Government.[16]

Culminating this period of ostensibly great friendship and cooperation, on January 4, 1919, just prior to the opening of the Paris Peace Conference, Emir Feisal and Chaim Weizmann signed a joint agreement (dated January 3) in the recognition "that the surest means of working out the consummation of their national aspirations, is through the closest possible collaboration in the development of the Arab State and Palestine," and in confirmation of "the good understanding which exists between them." The agreement, among other things, stipulated:

> Article I. The Arab State and Palestine in all their relations and undertakings shall be controlled by the most cordial goodwill and understanding and to this end Arab and Jewish duly accredited agents shall be established and maintained in their respective territories.

Article II. Immediately following the completion of the deliberations of the Peace Conference, the definite boundaries between the Arab State and Palestine shall be determined by a Commission to be agreed upon by the parties hereto.

Article III. In the establishment of the Constitution and Administration of Palestine all such measures shall be adopted as will afford the fullest guarantees for carrying into effect the British Governments Declaration of the 2nd of November, 1917.

Article IV. All necessary measures shall be taken to encourage and stimulate immigration of Jews into Palestine on a large scale, and as quickly as possible to settle Jewish immigrants upon the land through closer settlement and intensive cultivation of the soil. In taking such measures the Arab peasant and tenant farmers shall be protected in their rights, and shall be assisted in forwarding their economic development.[17]

There can be little if any serious doubt that this agreement recognizes the independence of Palestine from the Arab state (Syria) and the commitment to recognize Palestine as the Jewish homeland provided for under the Balfour Declaration. It is also true that Feisal appended a clause in Arabic below his signature which made the validity of the agreement as a whole conditional upon his receiving British assent to a set of demands he was forwarding to them at the time, something that did not happen. Since Hussein did not receive the necessary concurrence with his demands concerning an independent Arab state in Syria from the British, he felt that he had no further obligation to meet his commitments to the Zionists. Thus the agreement with Weizmann remained a dead letter. However, the fact that such an agreement was signed by Feisal in the first place clearly demonstrates, contrary to the arguments of his apologists, that the emir was fully aware of the implications of Zionist aims in Palestine. He understood quite well that the document he signed affirmed the separation of Palestine from the Arab state that he was attempting to build in Syria. There is plainly no way its language could be construed to mean anything else. It thus borders on the absurd to argue, as do some, that Feisal didn't really know what was going on, or what he had agreed to; that because he didn't know English himself and did not have a reliable translator, anything attributed to him either verbally or in writing that is recorded in English is not his but the voice and hand of T. E.

Lawrence.[18] It is also noteworthy that Feisal's disability in English and Lawrence's perfidy as his sometimes exclusive translator only affected matters concerned with the Zionists. There appear to have been no problems of this sort with regard to a whole host of sensitive matters that could not but be of at least equal if not far greater importance and sensitivity to Feisal.

Furthermore, it seems somewhat disingenuous for the authoritative historian of Arab nationalism, George Antonius, to suggest that

> Weizmann had given him an assurance that the Zionists had no intention of working for the establishment of a Jewish government in Palestine, but that all they wished to do was to help in the development of the country so far as that would be possible without damage to legitimate Arab interests. The combined effect of these assurances had been to induce in him a belief that there was nothing either in the Zionist aspirations as such or in the policy professed by the British Government in regard to their fulfillment that would interfere with Arab political and economic freedom in Palestine.[19]

This is to attribute to Feisal an incredible naiveté, and to castigate his closest advisers, both Arabs and Englishmen, as having deliberately allowed him to be misled, not only on January 4, 1919, but also for at least three years before then, since there was very little secret about what the Zionist aims were. Furthermore, in total contradiction of this argument is the fact that a week after the signing of the Weizmann-Feisal accord there was another meeting of Arab and Zionist leaders. At this meeting, the Zionist leaders offered the Arabs some significant concessions in compensation for their own claims. These concessions included a free zone in the port of Haifa and a joint free harbor in the Aqaba area.[20] What Feisal's apologists apparently cannot reconcile themselves to is the fact that the emir was never an Arab nationalist in the sense that the term was understood in Syria and Iraq. His ultimate goal was and remained that of building a Hashemite empire in as much of the Arab world as possible. He was thus quite willing to abandon Arab nationalist claims to Palestine as long as he thought he might be able to get Syria in exchange.

The Zionist claims for the boundaries of Palestine were formulated on the basis of detailed surveys and studies and postulated expert views regarding the indispensable territorial requirements for economic viability and national security. As these had been articulated publicly in detail since 1917, it was well known that the Zionists considered it essential for Palestine to encompass the water resources of the Litani River, the headwaters of the Jordan at Mount Hermon, and the Yarmuk River and its tributaries. These were deemed necessary to supply the level of hydroelectric power required to compensate for the lack of coal or oil in the country to fuel its future industries. The Transjordanian plateau and the Negev region were needed as the only areas of unoccupied lands that would be available for new large-scale Jewish settlement. From a security perspective, it was necessary to control the major invasion routes into the country, that is, the Bekaa Valley in the north and the deserts of the south and southwest, and Transjordan to the east at least as far as the Hejaz Railway.

Although the Zionist leaders held that all of Transjordania was part of Palestine and within the area covered by the Balfour Declaration, they limited their claims there to the Jordan Valley because of their sensitivity to Feisal's interests. On October 19, 1918, an article in *Palestine* acknowledged the strategic and religious importance of the Hejaz Railway to the emir and denied any Zionist claims to it as a gesture of friendship. The railway was in fact of crucial importance to Feisal as the only effective means of communication between Damascus and Medina. It thus provided a link to the Arab heartland that could serve to strengthen Syrian allegiance to the alien Hashemites, in addition to maintaining a connection with the Hashemite base in Hejaz. Furthermore, one of Feisal's main concerns with the Sykes-Picot Agreement was the fact that the French would have control of the coastal region, denying Feisal's Syria any direct access to the sea. The Zionist leaders recognized the validity of this concern and proposed to assure unimpeded access from Damascus to the port at Haifa and, if the Negev became Jewish, free access to the port at Aqaba as well. Feisal thus raised no objections to these proposed frontiers for Palestine when they were submitted to the Allied Supreme Council for consideration.

Indeed, on January 25, two of Feisal's principal aides, Abd al-Hadi and Ahmad Qadri, met with a Zionist representative in Paris and proposed the development of an Arab-Jewish entente that would undertake to determine the future of the two Semitic peoples among themselves. The Arab gambit, of course, was to try to get the Zionists to support them against an Anglo-French accommodation in Syria.[21] It was not long, however, before Feisal's pro-Zionist position of December 1918 and January 1919 began to waver. There is no evidence that Feisal met his personal commitment to support Zionist aspirations in Palestine before the Paris Peace Conference. In his appearance before the Supreme Council on February 6, 1919, Feisal would only go so far as to recommend that "Palestine, in consequence of its universal character, be left on one side for the mutual consideration of all parties concerned."[22] A more forthcoming position was taken a week later, on February 13, 1919, when a French-backed anti-Hashemite delegation from Le Comité Central Syrien of Paris headed by Chekri Ganem presented their case to the Supreme Council. They argued that the Syrians were not Arabs and pleaded for an independent and unified Syria under French protection.[23] As far as Palestine was concerned, they stated:

> Can we be permitted to say a word about Palestine, even though this is a painful topic for us? There can be no controverting the fact that Palestine is the southern part of our country. The Zionists demand it for themselves. We have suffered too much persecution, akin to the persecution they have suffered, not to open the gates of Palestine wide open to them. All of them who are suffering in reactionary countries will be welcomed. Let them settle in Palestine, but in an autonomous Palestine, linked with Syria only through a federation. Will not a Palestine that enjoys complete internal autonomy constitute sufficient guarantee for them? If they become a majority there, they will be the ones that rule. And if they are a minority, they will be represented in the government in proportion to their numbers. Is it necessary, in order to strengthen them, to split up Syria, to take away its hinterland and its historic safeguard against any invasion (which always took this route), and to establish a state in the center of a country, which, as a result, will always be hostile to it?[24]

It appears that during this period the French were using Ganem as an offset to Feisal, whose future rested in the hands of the British. To get the support of their sponsors, both were prepared to work out compromise arrangements with the Zionists in Palestine. It is noteworthy that neither gave any consideration whatever to the possibility of an independent, indigenous Palestinian Arab state.

On February 27, 1919, a Zionist delegation appeared before the Supreme Council and presented their program. Before they left, the American secretary of state, Robert Lansing, asked them for a definition of the phrase "a Jewish national home." Did that mean an autonomous Jewish government? Weizmann, speaking for the delegation, answered:

> The Zionist organization did not want an autonomous Jewish Government, but merely to establish in Palestine, under a mandatory Power, an administration, not necessarily Jewish, which would render it possible to send into Palestine 70 to 80,000 Jews annually. The Zionist Association would require to have permission at the same time to build Jewish schools, where Hebrew would be taught, and in that way to build up gradually a nationality which would be as Jewish as the French nation was French and the British nation British. Later on, when the Jews formed the large majority, they would be ripe to establish such a Government as would answer to the state of the development of the country and to their ideals.[25]

At the same time, while Feisal was in Paris, he gave an interview that was published in *Le Matin* on March 1, 1919. He was quoted as saying, "If the Jews desire to establish a state and claim sovereign rights in the country, I foresee and fear very serious dangers and conflicts between them and the other races." Weizmann and Felix Frankfurter quickly met with Feisal's secretary to determine whether Feisal was sending a signal that contravened the understandings reached earlier. It was explained that what Feisal actually said was, "If the Zionists wished to found a Jewish State at the present moment, they would meet with difficulties from the local population."[26]

Nonetheless, Feisal's published remarks in Paris created some consternation among the Zionist leadership. To put these concerns to rest, it was suggested that Feisal send a letter to Professor Felix Frankfurter, a member of the American Jewish delegation to the Peace Conference, outlining his position on

Hashemite-Zionist Cooperation

Zionist aspirations in Palestine. Feisal agreed to this proposal, primarily as a means of further bolstering his position on Syria through obtaining American support. Presumably, if Feisal were forthcoming on Palestine, the Americans would reciprocate by backing his claims in Syria against the French. The following letter, drafted by Feisal, T. E. Lawrence, Weizmann, Frankfurter and Colonel R. Meinertzhagen, was sent to Frankfurter in March 1919:

Dear Mr. Frankfurter:

I want to take this opportunity of my first contact with American Zionists to tell you what I have often been able to say to Dr. Weizmann in the past.

We feel that the Arabs and Jews are cousins in race, have suffered similar oppressions at the hands of powers stronger than themselves, and by a happy coincidence have been able to take the first step towards the attainment of their national ideals together.

We Arabs, especially the educated among us, look with the deepest sympathy on the Zionist movement. Our deputation here in Paris is fully acquainted with the proposals submitted yesterday by the Zionist Organization to the Peace Conference, and we regard them as moderate and proper. We will do our best, in so far as we are concerned, to help them get through: we will wish the Jews a most hearty welcome home.

With the chiefs of your movement, especially with Dr. Weizmann, we have had, and continue to have, the closest relations. He has been a great helper of our cause, and I hope the Arabs may soon be in a position to make the Jews some return for their kindness. We are working together for a reformed and revised Near East, and our two movements complete one another. The Jewish Movement is national and not imperialist, and there is room in Syria for both of us.

Indeed, I think that neither can be a real success without the other.

People less informed and less responsible than our leaders and yours, ignoring the need for cooperation of the Arabs and the Zionists, have been trying to exploit the local difficulties that must necessarily arise in Palestine in the early stages of our movements. Some of them have, I am afraid, misrepresented your aims to the Arab peasantry and our aims to the Jewish peasantry, with the result that interested parties have been enabled to make capital out of what they call our differences.

I wish to give you my firm conviction that these differences are not on questions of principle but matters of detail such as must inevitably occur in every contact of neighbouring peoples, and are as easily adjusted by mutual goodwill. Indeed nearly all of them will disappear with further knowledge.

I look forward and my people with me look forward to a future in which we will help you and you will help us, so that the countries in which we are mutually interested may once again take their place in the community of civilized peoples of the world.

Believe me, Yours sincerely,
(signed) Feisal[27]

It is of interest to note here the nature of the proposals submitted to the Paris Peace Conference by the Zionists that Feisal found to be "moderate and proper." The proposals, which were published in the London *Jewish Chronicle* on March 7, 1919, included the following claims:

> (a) The recognition of the historic title of the Jewish People in Palestine and the right of the Jews to reconstitute their National Home in Palestine:
> (b) That the Mandate shall be subject to the following special conditions:
> (i) Palestine is to be placed under such political, administrative and economic conditions as shall secure the establishment there of an autonomous Commonwealth; it being understood that nothing shall be done which may prejudice the civil and religious rights of existing non-Jewish communities in Palestine or the rights and political status enjoyed by Jews in any other country.
> (ii) To this end the Mandatory Power shall, inter alia: (i) Promote Jewish immigration and close settlement on the land, the established rights of the present non-Jewish population being equitably safeguarded. (ii) Accept the co-operation in all such measures as may from time to time be found necessary for carrying out the provisions of the Mandate, of a Council representative of the Jews of Palestine and the Jewries of the world, that is to be established for the development of the Jewish National Home in Palestine. . . .[28]

As suggested earlier, Feisal's enthusiasm and support for Zionist aspirations lasted only a short time. He soon learned that he had not only overestimated his own position as leader of the Arabs but had also failed to grasp the character of Arab nationalism. He seems to have adopted the rather naive notion that there was an identity of interest between Arab nationalism and the erection of a Hashemite Arab empire. He was to discover that the Hashemite leadership which he represented had never gained serious acceptance outside the Hejaz. Furthermore, he seemed to have forgotten that the British commitment to Arab national interests, at least insofar as the Declaration to the Seven of June 16, 1918, was concerned, was enunciated as a consequence of an appeal based on the disenchantment of the seven Syrian notables with the prospect of Hashemite domination of the Arab East. By 1919, Feisal's position in Damascus, notwithstanding his installation by Allenby as supreme administrator, remained tenuous. He could continue as the nominal leader of the Arabs only so long as what he did and said corresponded with the will and direction being pursued by the indigenous leadership of the Syrian nationalists. The moment he was perceived as doing otherwise, he reverted to the status of an alien Bedouin chief, virtually without a following in the country. Weizmann was therefore an exception among the Zionist leaders insofar as he took Feisal far more seriously than he was taken by most of the rest. They, and particularly the leaders from Palestine, who were far better informed as to true Arab opinion, took a far dimmer view of the significance of Feisal's promises and commitments. When he failed to follow through on them, there was no outcry or outrage from the Zionist leadership. They had never really placed much value on his influence among the Arabs in the first place.

As it became increasingly clear to Feisal that he would not be able to get the Zionists to intervene with the British and French on his behalf, he discontinued his contacts with them and even requested that they not refer to past statements he may have made that were favorable to Zionism. Interestingly, the Zionists basically conformed with his request. They saw no advantage to be gained by citing Feisal as a past friend. It could only embarrass him and work against any moderation he might try to bring to the increasingly radical Syrian Arab nationalists. It was out of this deference to the sensitivity of Feisal's position in Damascus that the Hussein-Weizmann agreement was not published by the Zionists until 1936.

Feisal was under increasing pressure from the more extreme elements in the Arab national movement, particularly with regard to Palestine. A report from the chief political officer in

Damascus, dated May 16, 1919, suggested that already at that early time, only some six months after having established his regime, Feisal had completely lost the ability to control or significantly influence the Arabs in Palestine. "Feisal is beginning to realise the difficulties which he will have in reconciling the Palestinians and the Zionists and no longer treats the question as a minor one. He has abandoned his idea of having a Conference here, but intends to ask various notables to visit him separately and endeavor to convert them. He will also try to induce the Zionist Commission to moderate its demands and will probably propose a conference to the Peace Commission."[29]

Indeed, Feisal did nothing to offset the resolution passed by the Syrian congress on July 2, 1919, and subsequently submitted to an American Commission of Inquiry (King Crane Commission) investigating the problem. That resolution stated, in part: "We reject the claims of the Zionists to the southern part of Syria, i.e., Palestine, which they wish to make into a national home for the Jews. We are opposed to their immigration into any part of our country because they do not have the slightest right thereto and because economically, ethnically, and politically they constitute a very grave danger to our existence."[30]

As reported to Lord Curzon in the summer of 1919 by a British intelligence officer in Egypt: "In my opinion, Dr. Weizmann's agreement with Emir Feisal is not worth the paper it is written on or the energy wasted in the conversation to make it. On the other hand, if it becomes sufficiently known among the Arabs, it will be somewhat in the nature of a noose about Feisal's neck, for he will be regarded by the Arab population as a traitor. No greater mistake could be made than to regard Feisal as a representative of Palestinian Arabs."[31] Again, on August 30, with a hint of compassion for the impossible situation in which Feisal found himself, the same officer reported, "The situation is exceedingly difficult for the Emir Feisal, whom I believe to have made honest attempts to hold the balance between the moderate and extreme sections of the Arabs and who desires to fulfill his promises both to His Majesty's Government and to the Zionists."[32]

Nevertheless, Feisal was becoming increasingly desperate as he began to understand that he was about to be abandoned by his British sponsors, who were simply handing him over to the

Hashemite-Zionist Cooperation

French. This was soon confirmed by the Anglo-French Agreement of September 15, 1919, that provided for the withdrawal of British forces from Syria and their replacement by French troops in Lebanon. Thus, according to a note from a British political officer writing from Damascus on September 25, 1919, Feisal's secret contacts with some favorably disposed Zionist leaders were continuing. Feisal apparently continued to cling to the vain hope that somehow the Zionists could be induced to come to his support against the French. Reporting on some recent conversations between Weizmann and Feisal, the officer stated:

> Weizmann has approached him and two long discussions have already taken place. I understand that Dr. Weizmann, in return for the Emir's help in Palestine towards the realization of Zionist aspirations, proposes to give money and advisers, if required, to the Arab Government and claims that the Zionists can persuade the French Government to waive their claims of influence in the interior. The Emir is strongly inclined to come to an agreement but matters are at present at a deadlock since the Emir asks the Zionists to throw in their lot definitely with the Arabs against the French, while Dr. Weizmann is in favour of allowing the French to occupy the coastal districts, saying that they can be squeezed out later.[33]

In the same vein, Weizmann wrote to Balfour on September 27:

> I have seen Feyzal and had a very long conference with him. . . . Feyzal does not like the French and is frightened of their interference. . . . He is in a difficulty as he cannot stand alone, he does not want the French and he cannot have the English or the Americans. . . . For this reason Feyzal would accept our help and advice. He is ready to take Jewish advisers and is willing, even anxious, to have Zionist support in the development and even administration of the Damascus region. . . . By cooperating with Feyzal we would gain the good will both of Damascus and Mecca, we would have peace in Syria and Palestine. . . . I have tried to see Lord Curzon and the Prime Minister, but so far I have failed.[34]

It was becoming increasingly apparent that the Hashemite-Zionist relationship was going nowhere. Feisal went to London in the fall of 1919 and gave an interview to the *Jewish Chronicle* that was published on October 3. In it, Feisal now repeated his opposition to the dismemberment of Palestine from Syria and warned against the dangers of Jewish-Arab clashes in Palestine because of extremist Jewish plans to take over the country and set up a Jewish state. On the other hand, he stated, "I found Dr. Weizmann's proposals quite moderate and practical. As I understand, he is working for a regulated immigration into the country, for conditions in which the Jew will have equal rights with the Arab, shall take part in the government of Palestine. . . . There is nothing to object to in that." It was clear that Feisal had fully accommodated himself to the Syrian nationalist position.

Nonetheless, a few of the leading British Zionists still attached some importance to Feisal, and a meeting with him was held in London at the Carlton Hotel on October 15. It was attended by Herbert Samuel, Harry Sacher, B. W. Cohen, and Said Pasha, Feisal's adjutant. Samuel asked whether the statements made in the interview had been correctly translated. Feisal then explained that the *Jewish Chronicle* correspondent had told him that the Zionists wanted to found a Jewish state in Palestine at once and had asked him whether he agreed to this. Feisal told the correspondent that he had never approved any such plan and that Dr. Weizmann had never raised it. To this the correspondent replied, "Dr. Weizmann is a politician. But what the Zionists really want is to establish a Jewish state in Palestine outright." Feisal replied to the effect that he could not agree that a small minority of Jews should rule a country most of whose inhabitants were Arabs. At that point, Samuel interrupted to point out that the Zionists had never demanded the *immediate* formation of a Jewish state. Feisal responded by stating that he had always been consistent in his attitude toward Zionism, which was reflected in his agreement with Weizmann and his letter to Frankfurter.

Samuel was apparently willing to accept the *Jewish Chronicle* incident as a misunderstanding between Feisal and the correspondent. The *Chronicle* denied this at once. It seems clear that Feisal was adjusting his statements to meet the expectations of his various audiences, without any great concern over consistency and to good effect. According to a British Foreign Office note of December 30, 1919, "Although some of Feisal's entourage dislike Zionism, Feisal himself and his most influential supporters are understood to realise that they can look to Zionism for sound advice with both men and especially money as an offset to the French."[35]

In the final analysis, Feisal had no option but to try to reach an acceptable agreement with the French over the future of Syria. That fall, he went to Paris to negotiate a treaty with French premier Clemenceau that would regularize the relations between France and Syria. Clemenceau recognized the enormous pressures that Feisal was under and apparently went out of his way to keep the French demands to an irreducible minimum. Having done this, he told Feisal, "I advise you to settle for this treaty and sign it while I'm in power; for I assure you that it is impossible for me to be followed by any government that would be even partially satisfied with what I am willing to accept now."[36] Feisal was in a dilemma. While he was personally inclined to go along with Clemenceau, his close advisers were sharply divided over the treaty. Feisal decided to stall until after he returned to Damascus and had a better sense of the public temper.

Feisal returned to Damascus in January 1920 after an absence of four months. Altogether, since the beginning of his regime in November 1918, he had been in Damascus for a total of about five months. He thus sacrificed the opportunity to shape events in Syria according to his own desired mold. As it was, he completely lost control of affairs. During his most recent absence, radical changes had taken place. British troops and advisers had been withdrawn in November 1919, and French troops had entered Lebanon. Without Feisal's presence to serve as a moderating influence, extremist agitation against the French, the British and even against Feisal and the Hashemites became rampant. The emir was accused of being first a British puppet and now a French agent. His sole recourse for political survival was effectively to join the extremist camp as a means of self-vindication.

On March 6, 1920, Feisal convened a Syrian General Congress which promptly repudiated the accommodation on Syria that he had just negotiated with Clemenceau, and on March 8 proclaimed the independence of a United Syria that included Lebanon and Palestine. It also elected Feisal to be the nation's constitutional monarch, and at the same time took the occasion also to proclaim the independence of Iraq, declaring Abdullah to be its king. Lord Curzon warned Feisal from London that not only would Britain not recognize him as king of Syria, it also rejected the competence of a group in Damascus to speak for Mesopotamia and Palestine. On March 22, a group of Lebanese Christian notables gathered and proclaimed an independent Lebanon. Nonetheless, Feisal continued to pretend that his monarchy was well established even as local disturbances continued to increase in the multiethnic and multireligious communities.

Feisal ensured the dangerous enmity of the French by reneging on the draft agreement that had been negotiated directly with the French premier, while at the same time losing a great deal of prestige among the Syrians because of the widespread knowledge that he had in fact made a deal with the French. At this critical time, information about his agreement of the previous year with Weizmann leaked out. Feisal was now accused of being in the pay of the Jews, their hired man in Damascus. To offset this impression, he lent the residual prestige of his name to extremist anti-Zionist propaganda and agitation which culminated in the sponsorship of attacks on Jewish settlements in northern Palestine. The attack at Tel Hai brought about the death of Joseph Trumpeldor of Zionist Mule Corps and Jewish Legion fame, a true Zionist folk hero. After this, Feisal lost all credibility among the Jewish leaders, who were outraged by his indirect role in the affair. Even Weizmann, who retained his confidence in Feisal and the British longer than any other major Zionist leader, reported from Palestine to the Zionist Executive in London on March 25, 1920, that "from the reports I am enclosing you will see that Allenby, and with him all the rest, practically agreed and perhaps encouraged Feyzal in his action. These gentlemen here have entirely forgotten about Zionism and have sold us over to Feyzal without the slightest compunction."[37]

The mounting instability in Syria placed the status and viability of the kingdom in serious question among numerous influential persons around Feisal. In particular, the disturbances that affected the Christian community could be expected to bring a severe and tangible French reaction. Some suggested that a possible solution might lie in a new relationship with the Turks. Since Turkey's defeat, the country had undergone dramatic change under Mustafa Kemal. Now might be the right time, they urged, for Feisal to align himself with the Turkish nationalist leader. At least the Turks were Muslims and would be easier to come to terms with. The Turks appeared to have conceded the loss of their empire and no longer posed a serious threat in that regard. They might welcome a new arrangement with a fellow Muslim state that would give them a new international position of respectability. For Syria, an arrangement with another Muslim state was surely preferable to the danger of rule by a centralist Catholic power such as France. Feisal, who from the very beginning maintained an affinity for continuing the Hashemite relationship with the Porte, authorized two prominent Syrians to go to Ankara and explore the feasibility of such an arrangement. The emissaries succeeded in working out a tentative arrangement whereby Syria and Turkey would unite in the same manner as Austria and Hungary had in the prewar Dual Monarchy. However, by the time Feisal's emissaries returned to Damascus in April, he had already adopted too extreme a stance along Arab nationalist lines for this kind of relationship to be viable. Later, in July 1920, when he was confronted with an imminent French invasion, Feisal was prepared to reverse himself, but he was already past the point of no return.[38]

Shortly after the Syrian National Congress declared Syria's independence and made Feisal king, the French and British decided it was time to dispose of the outstanding and increasingly nettlesome problems in the region. The Allied Supreme Council convened at San Remo, Italy, on April 19, and within a week hammered out an agreement on the disposition of the former Turkish imperial territories. On April 26, 1920, the Supreme Council unanimously assigned the mandate for Syria to France, while Britain became the mandatory power over Mesopotamia and Palestine. Syria and Mesopotamia were acknowledged as "provisionally independent" states under mandatory tutelage and control. As far as Palestine was concerned, the text of the mandatory award included the Balfour Declaration, thereby imposing an obligation on Britain to help bring about a viable national home for the Jews as part of its responsibility to the world community. The agreement on Palestine rejected the proposed Zionist frontiers and restored the border essentially to that previously negotiated under the Sykes-Picot Agreement, with the important exception that the international Brown Zone of the agreement was discarded and now formed an integral part of mandatory Palestine.

By his refusal to accept the diplomatic fait accompli of San Remo, Feisal found himself on a collision course with France. It was not long before his apparent inability to control the Syrian extremists, who had launched a spate of terror attacks against Maronite communities along the coast and were harassing French troops, precipitated the expected French reaction that had driven some of Feisal's advisers to seek a security arrangement with Turkey. However, it was not until Feisal committed the rash act of interdicting French use of the Rayak-Aleppo railroad, which was essential for bringing supplies to the French garrisons in Cilicia, that open war broke out. On July 14, the French sent Feisal a nonnegotiable ultimatum that effectively nullified Syria's independence and reduced it to a protectorate at best. Feisal had no alternative but to accept, and was encouraged to do so by the British. However, on the last day of the grace period, July 21, French forces marched into the Syrian interior and Feisal was presented with additional demands which amounted to a total surrender. Feisal knew he could not effectively resist the French. At the same time, however, he knew that his capitulation in the prevailing atmosphere of nationalist hysteria might well precipitate a civil war. He decided to hold out.

The truce ended on July 24, the day that became known in Syrian history as the Day of Maysalun, and the French forces attacked and promptly defeated the Syrian army. The French then reached and occupied Damascus on July 26 and quickly established order in the city. The following day, Feisal was given a letter that requested his departure from Damascus by special train on July 28. There were some administrative matters that delayed his departure until August 1. On that day, the notion of a Hashemite empire encompassing the Arab world was shattered beyond repair.

Feisal's expulsion from Syria was greeted with indifference by the Zionists. Regardless of whether he had been sincere in his protestations of sympathy for Zionist aspirations, he had proven himself unreliable and incapable of maintaining order and security in northern Palestine. Indeed, the very fact of the French presence in Damascus promised an immediate improvement of the security situation. On August 6, on his way to exile, Feisal met with David Eder of the Zionist Commission in Haifa. Feisal, now a king without a kingdom, was still interested in using the Zionists to salvage his situation. He stated that he knew that "the power of the Jewish press was great; could it not be mobilized in his favor?" Eder told him that he was mistaken; the pervasive influence of the Jewish press that he imagined did not exist. Eder did not dwell on the point. Instead, as he reported to Weizmann: "I had to point out to him [Feisal] he had tried to be too clever; he was a Zionist in Europe; he backed the anti-Zionists at Damascus; he was trying to play off the French against the English and *vice versa*. He must pursue a straightforward policy if there was to be any chance of success—the recognition of the Balfour Declaration and all its implications, which I detailed, in Palestine. He asked how we could help him and what we expected from him." Eder responded by advising Feisal that the Zionists wanted him to use his influence to bring the anti-Zionist propaganda to a halt, and "to recognise fully the Zionist influence in Palestine and to abandon all cries for a United Syria." He concluded his report with a personal assessment of Feisal: "I believe Feisal is still in favour with the British. The Arabs, including some of Feisal's entourage, attribute his defeat to the anti-Zionism of his extreme Party. I doubt, after studying Feisal during my interview whether he is strong enough to rule an Arab people.[39]

This last-minute maneuvering came to nothing. It was already too late to avert the conflict between the Zionists and the Arab nationalists over Palestine.

Unknown at the time to the Zionist leaders, Feisal had begun to make a bid for Palestine when it became apparent to him that he could not politically survive his collision with the French in Syria. He had objected to the appointment of Herbert Samuel as high commissioner because of the latter's Zionist connections and, in a meeting at the British Foreign Office with a representative of Lord Curzon on January 20, 1921, he claimed that Palestine had always been understood to be part of the McMahon pledge to Hussein. The implication of this was that Feisal should be given control of Palestine in exchange for the lost position originally given to him by Britain in Syria. Curzon took a dim view of Feisal's ideas. He thought it pointless to discuss the matter with Feisal, and absurd for Hussein to pretend that Britain was somehow obligated to consult him with regard to the disposition of either Mesopotamia or Palestine. "He did not conquer either country; we did. . . . The idea of a great unified Arab kingdom—never contemplated or promised by the Powers—though it may have existed in the brain of Hussein, has failed to materialise. Britain has taken the Mandate for Palestine . . . and it has been ratified at San Remo. It is not open to Hussein or Feisal to dispute it."[40]

Feisal's personal fortunes nonetheless took a dramatic turn for the better as a consequence of a long and bitter revolt that had shaken Iraq. It was decided by Britain, under its mandate for Mesopotamia, that it was necessary to place an Arab ruler over the country. The choice fell on the deposed king of Syria, Feisal, who was the only one believed sufficiently acceptable to the populace to be able to maintain order in the country. Accordingly, the throne was offered to Feisal, and on March 1, 1921, he was made king of Iraq by the British government.

4

The Emergence of Hashemite Transjordan

The Turkish government had never seriously attempted to bring the Bedouins that roamed Transjordan under firm control. Every once in a while, when a particularly egregious outrage was committed against another tribe or a settlement, the authorities might undertake a punitive expedition. For the most part, however, the territory, and most especially its southernmost areas, remained under the effective control of the Bedouins, who subjected the small settled population to raids and other excesses, such as demands for protection payments.

With the construction of the Hejaz Railway, which passed through it from north to south, the area took on a hitherto unknown strategic importance. Thus, when war broke out, the western part of Transjordan became an important military target, and much of the Arab contribution to the success of Allenby's campaign against the Turkish Fourth Army consisted in keeping the railroad inoperative. For a short period, the presence of British military forces there brought about a general condition of order. With the conclusion of the war, however, Transjordan lost its strategic significance and was treated with benign neglect by both the British authorities and the civil regime of Feisal based in Damascus. The British were deeply embroiled with the French over the delimitation of the latter's zone in Lebanon and Syria and, to resolve the issues between them, made a number of concessions that seriously affected Zionist territorial aspirations. Under one such concession, the British were to withdraw their forces from the coastal zone in Syria and from the Arab zone under Feisal's administration north of the Yarmuk. Transjordan was to remain under British occupation. However, Curzon, who replaced Balfour as foreign secretary, was concerned that Clemenceau would use the ongoing British occupation of the Arab zone south of the Yarmuk, that is, Transjordan, as an excuse for the military occupation of Syria, which would be disastrous for the Feisal regime in Damascus and the British strategic interests for which his rule was established in the first place. The British were determined to prevent the French from gaining control over the north-south railroad that passed through the Syrian towns of Damascus, Hama, Homs and Aleppo. Were such to happen, the French would have a significant advantage over the British in the ability to mobilize and concentrate military forces for action in the region. Accordingly, in the middle of 1919, the British decided temporarily to withdraw their forces from Transjordan. The immediate consequence of this was a reversion of the territory to a state of anarchy that directly interfered with Zionist plans for establishing settlements there, as noted by Weizmann in a communication to Herbert Samuel in November 1919.[1]

The problem of security and stability was further exacerbated by the estrangement that had been growing between Hussein and Feisal. While the former had continued to hold to his dream of a vast Hashemite empire, Feisal soon recognized that such was not going to come into being and therefore accepted the throne of Syria for himself when it was offered by the Syrian National Congress. While he made no serious attempt to administer the territory of Transjordan from Damascus, he did make an occasional gesture designed to demonstrate and thereby justify his claim to jurisdiction over the territory. At the same time, Hussein, who claimed it as part of the kingdom of Hejaz, made contradictory gestures. Thus it came about that while a governor appears to have been appointed in Aqaba, no one was quite sure as to whom he was responsible, since he received occasionally conflicting instructions from both Hussein in Mecca and Feisal in

Damascus. As a consequence, he tended to ignore both and do as he pleased. Adding to the confusion, Damascus appointed a governor at Ma'an. At the same time, the governor at Aqaba was instructed by Mecca to take control of Ma'an as part of his jurisdiction.[2] It was to be some time before the Hejaz-Transjordan border was delineated.

In the summer of 1920, when Feisal was forced out of Syria by the French, the situation in Transjordan deteriorated rapidly. Transjordan, which was part of the Palestine Mandate assigned to Britain at the San Remo Conference the previous April, became in essence a no-man's-land whose 300,000 peasants and semi-nomads were ruled by local sheikhs who did as they pleased. The British were unsure of how to deal with the situation. On the one hand, they were unwilling to commit the military forces necessary to hold a territory of little consequence to them. On the other hand, the Bedouins, emboldened by the general anarchy and confusion, began to mount an increasing number of attacks on Jewish settlements west of the Jordan River. This posed a direct threat to the stability that the British were trying to institute in Palestine. Furthermore, the growing instability of Transjordan, coupled with the fact that many of Feisal's followers and dissident Syrian nationalists took refuge there after his expulsion from Damascus, raised the possibility of a French intervention in order to prevent the prevailing turmoil from spilling over into Syria.

On August 7, 1920, Herbert Samuel, the recently appointed high commissioner in Palestine, cabled London requesting permission to include Transjordan directly under his administration in order to institute order there. This would remove the risk of a French attempt to control the region from Damascus. London, however, was still unwilling to commit significant resources to an area it considered a backwater. Furthermore, the insurrection against the British in Mesopotamia made the government very wary of getting further entangled in direct rule over Arab territories. Thus, the response from Lord Curzon proposed instead that

> the first step should be to send a few suitable political officers to such places as Salt and Kerak, provided that no military escorts are necessary to ensure their safety. . . . The duties of these officers should be confined

to encouraging local self-government and to giving such advice as is asked for by the people. They should assist in the formation of municipal and district self-governing bodies and lose no opportunity of encouraging trade with Palestine and of emphasizing the fact that Palestine is the natural outlet for Trans-Jordania. . . . There must be no question of setting up any British Administration in that area and all that may be done at present is to send a maximum of four or five political officers.[3]

London's policy having been set forth, it only remained for Samuel to carry it out, notwithstanding his concerns about its practicability. On August 21, the high commissioner went to Salt to address a gathering of some six hundred notables who, as he later reported, indicated a desire that Britain establish an administration that would assure stability and security in the territory. Accordingly, in the summer of 1920, a few British Arabic-speaking officers together with some local Arab elders set up a number of local governments in the area of northern Transjordan between Kerak and Irbid. The most important of these were the "National Government of Moab" in Kerak under Alec Kirkbride, and the "Government of Amman" a few miles further north under his younger brother Alan. Another arrangement was worked out in the Ajlun area where Major Somerset negotiated the Umm Qeis Treaty with some local sheikhs on September 2, 1920. A fourth such local government was set up at Salt under the guidance of Major Camp. These governments, however, were without any real power and were incapable of exercising control over the large area entrusted to them. To make matters worse, the British officials assigned to them were given to understand that they would be wasting their time if they asked for any assistance from the British government that involved money or troops. The raids across the Jordan continued to increase, and Transjordan had also become the base for nationalist raids into Syria, which stirred up the French. They demanded that Britain pacify Transjordan, indicating that unless such was done soon, France would undertake the task itself.

It was thus clear at the time that as far as Britain and France, as well as most others, were concerned, Transjordan was part of Palestine, and was included within the British mandate over the latter. Indeed, there appears to have been a British plan, never

The Emergence of Hashemite Transjordan

advanced to the point of being formulated on paper, to use the territory as a reserve for Arabs to relocate to as the Zionist program in Palestine began to be achieved and the country was transformed into a Jewish dominated and ruled entity. As noted by Alec Kirkbride:

> His Majesty's Government were too busy setting up a civil administration in Palestine proper, west of the river Jordan, to be bothered about the remote and undeveloped areas which lay to the east of the river and which were intended to serve as a reserve of land for use in the resettlement of Arabs once the National Home for the Jews in Palestine, which they were pledged to support, became an accomplished fact. There was no intention at that stage of forming the territory east of the river Jordan into an independent Arab state.[4]

There was also good reason to believe that Hashemite ambition lay behind a good deal of the instability in the region. Samuel sent an urgent message to the War Office on September 21 with the information that King Hussein had made an appeal to the sheikhs of Kerak, Adwan and the Balka to prepare for an uprising under the leadership of one of his sons. The appeal stated in part: "This is the time to show your ardor and zeal in connection with your religion and country. Be united and assist your co-religionists to a deliverance of our country from the infidels. One of my sons is proceeding to you with funds and provisions."[5] A week later there was a complaint from the French that Hussein's sons, Ali and Abdullah, were planning an attack on Deraa. They indicated their concern that effective preventive actions be taken by the British.

Abdullah, sorely disappointed that he had been rejected by the British as leader of the Arab delegation to the Paris Peace Conference in favor of his younger brother Feisal, and in disfavor with his father because of disagreements on the handling of problems in the Arabian peninsula, saw the expulsion of Feisal as an opportunity to project the Hashemites once again onto the center stage of the Arab movement. In the autumn of 1920, he set out from Medina with an army of uncertain size, but reputed to have consisted of some two thousand tribesmen, and headed toward the town of Ma'an where he arrived on November 5.

Ma'an, about 150 miles south of Amman, was at the time still considered part of the Hejaz. Abdullah was preceded by a wave of rumors regarding his intentions. These were confirmed at Ma'an, where he announced his intention of marching through Transjordan to Damascus, where he was going to attack and expel the French and restore the throne to his brother Feisal.

Abdullah proceeded slowly and cautiously, waiting to see what the British reaction would be. The British requested that Feisal, who was in London at the time for talks about his own future, intervene with Abdullah to cease any provocative actions. Notwithstanding Feisal's assurances, High Commissioner Samuel warned London of the problems that would arise if Abdullah proclaimed a sherifian government over Transjordan. "If such an event took place the consequences which I have repeatedly pointed out . . . must ensue. Inter-tribal disorder and recurrence of raids into Palestine together with insecurity of Palestine's chief source of food supply would threaten serious re-action here."[6]

In January 1921 it was reported in Kerak that Abdullah was advancing toward the town at the head of his army. Kirkbride, who had a force of only fifty policemen and did not know what to do, appealed to Samuel for instructions. Several weeks later the following reply was received from Jerusalem: "It is considered most unlikely that the Emir Abdullah would advance into territory which is under British control."[7] Included in the response were instructions, a masterpiece of bureaucratic gibberish, on how the political officers were to conduct themselves in the event of "untoward and/or unforeseen circumstances":

> Your actions in the circumstances above adumbrated should be guided by the following considerations—
> that the duty laid upon you in Transjordania has been that of promoting local self-government and the maintenance of law and security;
> that if owing to the direct or indirect action of the population in whose interests you are working the possibility of carrying out those duties is denied you it is no longer incumbent upon (and obviously impossible for) you to remain at your post;
> that it would nevertheless be your duty to do all that you can (in the circumstances envisaged) to maintain law and order and dissuade the population (within the limits of the means at your disposal) from breaking it;

that in the event of your being unable to do so and bearing in mind the circumstances of your mission you should avoid allowing yourselves to be drawn into participation in hostilities and/or falling into the hands of the hostile party;

that even should no hostility be offered to yourselves personally you should be careful to avoid any action, overt or covert, of a nature prejudicial or hostile to the French or French interests.[8]

Two days later, Abdullah's force marched into British-controlled Moab. Unable to stop Abdullah, Kirkbride decided to welcome him instead. He, along with the National Government of Moab, went to meet Abdullah at the nearest station along the Hejaz Railway. With Abdullah's arrival, the National Government of Moab went out of existence. Buoyed by his success, Abdullah decided to proceed on to Amman. By March 1921, he and his "army" had effectively occupied all of Transjordan.

This audacious move by Abdullah placed the Colonial Office under Winston Churchill, which had just taken over Middle Eastern affairs from the Foreign Office, on the horns of a dilemma. On March 1, Weizmann sent a letter to Churchill in which he expressed concern about developments in Transjordan. He went on to restate and reaffirm Zionist claims to the area of Transjordan west of the Hejaz Railway, an area that had always been considered by the British government as an essential part of Palestine.[9] As an initial step in assuming responsibility for the Middle East, Churchill had organized a conference of regional political officers which began its deliberations in Cairo on March 12. By the time the Palestine Political and Military Committee, chaired by Churchill, met on March 17, Abdullah and his force were already in Amman.

The British authorities had previously reached a general consensus that, even though Transjordan came under the Palestine Mandate and was considered by the Zionists to be part of the territorial context for the development of the Jewish National Home, it was inadvisable to allow Zionist settlement to cross the Jordan since it would impose a heavy and costly security burden on the British authorities. On the other hand, Herbert Samuel, the high commissioner for Palestine, was opposed to the idea of making Transjordan a separate and independent Arab state. He argued further that Abdullah could not be allowed to take control of Transjordan and use it as a base for organizing military attacks against Syria. The question was, how to stop him? There seemed to be only two options. Either the British army had to be sent in to evict Abdullah from Transjordan, or the French had to be allowed to cross the frontier to accomplish that task. Both options were clearly unacceptable. The British government was unlikely to go to the expense of sending an army to fight in Transjordan, and it was equally unlikely that British policy would permit a French occupation of the area.

There was, however, another possibility suggested by Churchill. He argued that it was most important that the ruler of Transjordan be compatible with that of Iraq, since British strategy called for a direct overland link between Egypt and the Persian Gulf. Since Feisal had been given the throne of Iraq, it might be well to make his brother Abdullah ruler of Transjordan, or to appoint a Bedouin leader approved by him. The simplest and least costly alternative would be to accept Abdullah's fait accompli and make the most of it. Let Abdullah and his army act as an arm of the British mandate and maintain order in the unruly territory. The Cabinet was hesitant about the prospect of having Abdullah rule Transjordan on behalf of the British. A primary concern was the expected negative reaction of the French who, after finally expelling Feisal from Syria, would now find themselves virtually surrounded by Hashemite rulers under British patronage. In addition, there was the question of whether Abdullah would comply with British expectations of him. Churchill responded to the effect that he was not particularly interested in making Abdullah ruler, but that it was necessary to have him agree to whoever was to be chosen so as not to antagonize Feisal in Iraq. Before making up his mind, Churchill decided to go to Jerusalem and meet Abdullah in person.

Abdullah was invited by Samuel to come to Jerusalem to meet with Churchill on May 27, 1921. The meetings went on for three days. Churchill outlined the British proposals, which numbered seven. First, Abdullah would make sure that no actions against the French in Syria would be launched from Transjordan; second, Abdullah would renounce all rights to and claims against the throne of Iraq; third, he would establish and maintain order in

The Emergence of Hashemite Transjordan

Transjordan; fourth, he would recognize the British mandate over Transjordan as part of the Palestine Mandate, and would establish a government to administer the territory on behalf of and in the name of the mandatory power; fifth, he would receive a monthly subsidy of five thousand pounds for six months while the high commissioner worked out arrangements for a Transjordanian government and the appointment of an acceptable governor; sixth, the high commissioner would send a representative to Amman who would serve as adviser to Abdullah's government; finally, the British government would undertake to recognize the independence of Transjordan at some unspecified time in the future.[10]

Abdullah accepted the British proposals without qualification. It was clear to him that even though he was ostensibly the king designate of Iraq according to the proclamation of the Iraqi nationalists in Damascus in 1920, he was unacceptable in that capacity to the British, who preferred to see his brother Feisal on the throne in Baghdad. This would be Abdullah's last opportunity to gain a throne for himself. The British came to understand years later that Abdullah had no intention of doing anything as foolhardy as attacking the French in Syria. However, had he announced that he was simply taking over Transjordan, the British would most likely have kicked him out. As it was, they were quite ready to give it to him as compensation for not complicating their relations with the French. The arrangement was supposed to have been for a six-month period during which Abdullah was to restore order to the territory.

The new arrangement for Transjordan was not without its problems from the British perspective. Abdullah, administrator of Transjordan since March 1921, was before long viewed by both the Palestine administration and the Colonial Office as incapable and unreliable. By June, there a virtual consensus that Abdullah should go. The question was how to get rid of him in a politically acceptable manner. In the summer of 1921, T. E. Lawrence went to the Hejaz at the instance of Churchill to negotiate an agreement with the increasingly erratic Hussein. While there, he was to smooth the way for a return of Abdullah to Hussein's court. On his way, Lawrence presented Samuel with his views on Transjordan, the main thrust of which was that Transjordan should be united with Palestine. However, since the government was opposed to sending military forces to Transjordan, such a union could only be brought about peacefully if the Transjordanians agreed. It was Lawrence's judgment that Abdullah's continued misrule would accomplish that if he were left in place a while longer.[11] The ambivalence regarding Abdullah ultimately became resignation, and no actions were taken to remove him. His temporary position in Transjordan soon became a permanent arrangement when it was confirmed later that same year by the high commissioner.

The British resolution of the Transjordan problem nonetheless represented a significant departure from previous understandings between the British and the Zionists. In a memorandum to Lloyd George from Balfour dated June 26, 1919, dealing with the question of the disposition of former Turkish territories, the foreign secretary wrote:

> In determining the Palestinian frontiers, the main thing to keep in mind is to make a Zionist policy possible by giving the fullest scope to economic development in Palestine. Thus the Northern frontier should give to Palestine a full command of the water power which geographically belongs to Palestine and not to Syria; while the Eastern frontier should be so drawn as to give the widest scope to agricultural development on the left bank of the Jordan, consistent with leaving the Hedjaz Railway completely in Arab possession.[12]

Again on August 11, Balfour stated that "Palestine should extend into the lands lying east of the Jordan. It should not, however, be allowed to include the Hedjaz Railway which is too distinctly bound up with exclusively Arab interests."[13] Indeed, even Abdullah apparently experienced astonishment at this basic shift in Britain's position. He exclaimed: "He [God] granted me success in creating the Government of Transjordan by having it separated from the Balfour Declaration which had included it since the Sykes-Picot Agreement assigned it to the British zone of influence."[14]

The arbitrary British creation of an Arab emirate of Transjordan required a previously nonexisting legal framework to be constructed to allow this new entity to be recognized formally.

The Emergence of Hashemite Transjordan

Colonel Meinertzhagen noted in his diary on June 21, 1921: "The Colonial Office and the Palestine Administration have now declared that the articles of the mandate relating to the Jewish Home are not applicable to Transjordan and that the severance of Transjordan from Palestine is in accordance with the terms of the McMahon pledge. This discovery was not made until it became necessary to appease an Arab Emir."[15] The first draft of the Palestine Mandate had been submitted to the Council of the League of Nations by Balfour on December 6, 1920. There was nothing in that document that would provide the basis for distinguishing Transjordan from the rest of Palestine. Of course, this was before Abdullah's appearance on the scene in Transjordan and Britain's decision to strike a bargain with him. Accordingly, a new draft was released in August 1921 which accommodated this change in British policy. In this revised final draft of the League of Nations Mandate for Palestine, a device was included which provided the ex post facto basis for Britain's separation of Transjordan from Palestine. Article 25 provided that "in the territories lying between the Jordan and the eastern boundary of Palestine as ultimately determined, the Mandatory shall be entitled, with the consent of the Council of the League of Nations, to postpone or withhold application of such provisions of this mandate as he may consider inapplicable to the existing local conditions, and to make such provision for the administration of the territories as he may consider suitable to those conditions. . . ."

Notwithstanding the new version of the mandate, the Zionist leadership at the time never considered the exclusion of Transjordan from the Jewish homeland as final. That same year, at the Twelfth Zionist Congress, Weizmann stated, in discussion of the question of Palestine's eastern frontier, that "the question will be still better answered when Cisjordania is so full of Jews that a way is forced into Transjordania."[16]

On July 24, 1922, the League of Nations approved the terms of the British mandate covering Palestine and Transjordan. Kirkbride noted, with tongue in cheek, "In due course, the remarkable discovery was made that the clauses of the mandate relating to the establishment of the National Home for the Jews had never been intended to apply to the mandated territory east of the river."[17] However, Lawrence had noted, as an adviser to

Churchill, that the decisions to be reached at the Cairo Conference had all been prepared in advance. "It was decided to include Trans-Jordan in Palestine, to make it indistinguishable from Palestine and to open it to Jewish immigration. Every point was decided at Cairo as originally settled in London except the one about Trans-Jordan."[18] On September 16, 1922, Lord Balfour presented a memorandum requesting the consent of the Council of the League, as provided for in Article 25 of the mandate, to the exemption of Transjordan from all the clauses of the mandate concerned with the establishment of a Jewish National Home, including the mandatory's obligation to facilitate Jewish immigration and land settlement. With the council's assent, the imprimatur of the international community was given to the arbitrary partition of Palestine.

The following month, Abdullah, accompanied by his advisers, arrived in London to negotiate a final settlement of the status of Transjordan. The country was populated mostly by Bedouins, and it sorely needed skilled personnel, initiative, development and, most especially, capital investment. Abdullah believed that these might be forthcoming from the Jewish immigration into Palestine if he could but come to some agreement with the Zionists. During his London visit, he met five times with Weizmann and some of the latter's associates, trying to determine whether it would be possible to get Zionist support for his extension of the emirate to cover all of Palestine in exchange for his guarantee of support for the implementation of the Balfour Declaration and the Jewish National Home policy. The reports of these conversations indicated that Abdullah's proposal was in fact greeted with approval by the members of the Zionist Executive that participated in the meetings with him. The Zionist leaders stipulated, however, that the plan had to have the approval of Britain before they could agree to it. The British, for reasons of their own, which probably included the consideration that such an alliance could well result in Transjordan becoming too self-sufficient and therefore less compliant with British goals in the territory, would not agree and the initiative came to nothing.[19]

Once reports of the secret Abdullah-Weizmann meetings leaked out, both leaders were subjected to a torrent of criticism from their respective constituencies. Palestinian Arab leaders were suspicious of the new Hashemite ruler of Transjordan, fearing he might be as ready to sell their interests to further his own as his brother Feisal had been. On the Zionist side, David Ben-Gurion took sharp issue with Weizmann, who had "failed once with Feisal" and who "must be careful not to do the same this time" with Abdullah. Nevertheless, the Zionist leaders were anxious to find someone who could represent the Arabs with whom they might be able to negotiate a modus vivendi. Weizmann thought initially that perhaps Abdullah might be such an Arab leader. His assessment of Abdullah a few months later indicated that he no longer harbored any such illusions. In February 1923, Weizmann reported that it was "very doubtful whether the Emir carries any weight in Palestine or even in Trans-Jordania itself, and whether his promises and guarantees do represent an asset of any real value."[20]

On April 25, 1923, Herbert Samuel declared in Amman, in the name of the British government, that: "subject to the approval of the League of Nations, His Majesty's Government would recognize the existence of an independent government in Transjordan under the rule of His Highness the Amir Abdullah; provided that such government was constitutional and placed His Britannic Majesty's Government in a position to fulfill its international obligations in respect of the territory by means of an agreement to be concluded between the two Governments."[21] Although Abdullah announced the independence of Transjordan on May 25, 1923, it was still to take more than two decades before independence became a reality. On February 20, 1928, Britain signed a treaty with Abdullah that recognized the existence of an "independent government" in Transjordan. However, this independence was more ephemeral than real. Article 2 of the treaty stated: "The powers of legislation and of administration entrusted to His Britannic Majesty as Mandatory for Palestine shall be exercised in that part of the area under Mandate known as Trans-Jordan by His Highness the Emir through such constitutional government as is defined and determined in the Organic Law of Trans-Jordan and any amendment thereof made with the approval of His Britannic Majesty."[22] In addition, the emir had to agree to be advised in matters relating to foreign affairs, finance and fiscal policy, and jurisdiction over foreigners, by the British resident in Amman, who was under the British high commissioner for Palestine.

It was not long before the British began to exploit the opportunity presented by the arrangement with Transjordan for consolidating their influence in the Middle East. It was Herbert Samuel who, from his vantage point as high commissioner, served as the architect of British influence in Transjordan. In his view, it was better situated for British purposes than Palestine, since there was no Zionist problem there to complicate matters. It was a marriage of convenience. After 1922, when the British decided to channel their air routes to Iraq and India across Transjordan, the country became an important link in the imperial structure. Royal Air Force bases were built at Amman and Ziza, and the RAF assumed responsibility for the security of the territory. In exchange for his cooperation, Abdullah got the subsidy he needed to stay solvent.

Notwithstanding the arbitrary British action, the Thirteenth Zionist Congress (August 1923) included the following among its resolutions: "Recognizing that eastern and western Palestine are in reality and de facto one unit historically, geographically, and economically, the Congress expresses its expectation that the future of Transjordan shall be determined in accordance with the legitimate demands of the Jewish people."[23]

On August 18, 1926, Abdullah made basically the same argument, although without reference to the legitimacy of Zionist aspirations, when he stated:

> Palestine is one unit. The division between Palestine and Transjordan is artificial and wasteful. We, the Arabs and the Jews, can come to terms and live together in peace in the whole country, but you will have difficulty in reaching an understanding with Palestinian Arabs. You must make an alliance with us, the Arabs of Iraq, Transjordan, and Arabia. We are poor and you are rich. Please come to Transjordan. I guarantee your safety. Together we will work for the benefit of the country.[24]

Abdullah had come to realize that the future of his emirate was not very bright, given its very limited economic development potential. This accounted for his attempts, as well as those of some of the land-holding sheikhs, to interest the Jews from across the Jordan in participating in the agricultural development of Transjordan. In 1931, the legislative council passed a law granting Abdullah personal control of approximately 67,000 dunams of land that was previously the property of the Turkish sultan, 62,000 of which were underdeveloped vacant plots in the Jordan Valley. Unable to interest foreign investors in developing these lands, Abdullah turned, first through agents and then directly, to the Jewish Agency in Jerusalem. The negotiations culminated in an options agreement that was to hold for six to twelve months. The terms called for a thirty-three-year lease that could be renewed twice for a total of ninety-nine years. The annual payment was to be 2,200 Palestine pounds and five percent of any profits.[25] The negotiations and the agreement were kept secret. However, once the information was prematurely publicized by the local press in Palestine, a storm of protest developed among both the Palestinian Arabs and the British authorities. Under extreme pressure from these sources, including a direct personal appeal from Haj Amin al-Husseini, the mufti of Jerusalem, Abdullah reluctantly allowed the Arabic press to announce the cancellation of the agreement.

Notwithstanding the uproar over leasing lands in Transjordan to Palestinian Jews, many of the sheikhs were anxious to do precisely that. A meeting with Jewish leaders was held in Jerusalem on April 8, 1933. Representatives from Transjordan included Sheikh Mithqal Pasha al-Faiz, Chief of the Sakhr; Rashid Pasha al-Khaza'i, supreme sheikh at Mount Ajlun; Mitri Pasha Zurikat, leader of the Christian community at Kerak; Shams-ud-Din Bey Sami, leader of the Circassian community; Salim Pasha Abu al-Ajam, supreme sheikh of the Balka region; and Muhammad Abu-Khalid of Amman. The gathering focused on cooperation between the Zionists in Palestine and the Transjordanians. In concluding the discussions, Weizmann told the gathering, "The work we shall now begin will be like digging a tunnel in the hills. Both sides must start tunnelling—you from one end, and we from the other, until we meet in the middle." In responding on behalf of the Transjordanians, Shams-ud-Din Bey Sami said, with considerable prescience, "The excavation of the tunnel that Dr. Weizmann referred to is not, in my opinion, too difficult, and with joint effort the diggers can manage to meet. But I fear that in the middle of the mountain we shall run into a steel partition that will prevent our meeting. This partition is the British government. Dr. Weizmann is charged with the burdensome task of removing this partition. If he succeeds peace will be assured and established on firm foundations."[26] Weizmann, however, was not able to overcome British opposition to Zionist-Transjordanian cooperation. Indeed, the British had applied considerable pressure on Transjordan's legislative council to enact a law prohibiting the sale of land to Jews. In early 1933 the council rejected such a law by an overwhelming majority. The council wished to demonstrate its desire and commitment to an open door policy for Jewish development assistance. Eventually, the British succeeded in getting the council to enact a nationality law which had the desired effect, by not permitting land to be sold to foreigners.[27] The dissatisfaction with this restrictive practice was clearly reflected in an article published in *Mira'at-Ash-Sharq* on May 1, 1935:

> What do Palestinian Arabs think, when they ask Transjordanian Arabs not to sell their lands? Do they think Transjordan is inhabited by "superior beings" who can withstand the temptation? The people see how the Arabs of Palestine live in comfort, while they, the residents of Transjordan, are subject to poverty and hunger. If you think the Transjordanian Arabs will object to the Jews, you are mistaken. There is a limit to everything. . . . The people of Transjordan will be the first to demand the abrogation of the law forbidding foreigners to buy land in Transjordan, for they cannot exist without foreign capital.[28]

From the start of his career in Transjordan, Abdullah harbored his father's dream of a great Hashemite Arab empire, with an appropriate role carved out for himself. With the passing of Hussein, Abdullah envisioned himself as the ruler of a new Greater Syria that was to include Lebanon, Transjordan and Palestine. Following the death of Feisal in 1933, the vision was expanded to include Iraq as well. Abdullah's ambitions met with resistance throughout the Arab world. The politicians in Damascus had no interest in surrendering their purported leadership of the Arab movement to Abdullah, making Syria an appendage of Transjordan. Similarly, his ideas found little favor in Iraq which, as the largest and wealthiest of the Arab countries, was seen by its politicians as the natural leader of the Arab world. As for Ibn Saud, who had but recently succeeded in eliminating the Hashemite kingdom of the Hejaz and uniting most of the Arabian peninsula under the Saudi banner, he had no interest whatever in any scheme that would enhance the prestige of the defeated Hashemites. Finally, Abdullah's scheme was vehemently opposed by some of the Arab leaders in Palestine, most particularly the mufti of Jerusalem, Haj Amin al-Husseini, whose own ambitions conflicted with it.

The mufti also harbored dreams of liberating Palestine from the British and then expanding outward to create an Arab empire under his own leadership. Abdullah was thus seen by him as an obstacle to be overcome. On the other hand, the local opposition to the mufti, particularly the influential Nashashibis, seemed quite willing to see Abdullah as king of Palestine with British backing.

The increasing tension between the British and the Arab nationalists in Palestine, who were represented by the Arab Higher Committee formed in April 1936 by the mufti, presented the first serious opportunity for Abdullah to advance his ambitions. A Royal Commission was sent by London to investigate the disturbances that had rocked the country. In its report that was made public on July 7, 1937, the commission concluded that the only practicable solution to the intercommunal strife in Palestine was a partitioning of the country. It proposed that

> treaties of Alliance should be negotiated by the Mandatory with the Government of Trans-Jordan and representatives of the Arabs of Palestine on the one hand and with the Zionist Organization on the other. These Treaties would declare that, within as short a period as may be convenient, two sovereign independent States would be established—the one an Arab State, consisting of Trans-Jordan united with that part of Palestine which lies to the east and south of a frontier such as we suggest in Section 3 below; the other a Jewish State consisting of that part of Palestine which lies to the north and west of that frontier.[29]

The commission's report could not but have elated Abdullah. Here was Britain offering to expand his territory on its own initiative. However, it would not do to gloat over this in public, and Abdullah accordingly reacted with caution. He could not be seen as accepting the deal with alacrity as this might suggest an abandonment of Arab claims to all of Palestine, something that was anathema to most Arab nationalists. He thus indicated his reluctant acceptance of the partition scheme, if there were no other option for restoring order to the country. The prime minister of Iraq, however, roundly condemned the proposal and, with obvious reference to Abdullah, anyone who supported it: "Any person venturing to act as head of such a state would be regarded as an outcast throughout the Arab world, and would incur the wrath of Muslims all over the East. I declare, both as head of an Arab government and as a private citizen, that I shall always oppose any individual ready to stab the Arab race to the heart in order to secure the rulership of the proposed new state."[30] The Palestine Arab Higher Committee rejected the partition proposal. Nonetheless, later that year, W. Ormsby-Gore, representing Britain, appeared before the Permanent Mandates Commission of the League of Nations and stated that "he had every reason to believe that, for national and possibly other reasons, the Arabs of Trans-Jordan—not only the Amir Abdullah who had come out in favour of it—would like a larger state, would like independence, and regarded the proposal favorably." In June 1938, Abdullah wrote to the Young Muslim Association: "Since the people of Palestine have confined themselves to making protests, I have considered it my duty under my religion according to which I worship God and as something enjoined upon me by my racial affiliation, to strive to ward off the calamity by bringing about the union of Palestine and Transjordan." And to demonstrate his disinterestedness, he added, "The inhabitants of Palestine are 100,000 more than those of Transjordan and would ably take over the leadership of the administration of such a state."[31]

To Abdullah's disappointment, opposition to the partition plan was so strong that the British government relented and abandoned the scheme as unworkable. After the outbreak of World War II, Abdullah was to try in 1940 to get Britain to agree to a union of Syria and Transjordan, but the British suggested that he defer raising the matter until after the war was over. He tried to raise the issue again in 1941 and 1942, but to no avail. At the same time he recognized that the fact that Transjordan was still under the British mandate weakened his position as an advocate of Arab unity under his leadership. Thus, as the war was coming to a close, Abdullah began pressing the British for independence.

At the same time, the Zionists had not yet accepted the legitimacy of Transjordan as an independent entity. On January 24, 1946, Moshe Shertok (Sharett), then head of the political department of the Jewish Agency, stated:

> We have looked forward to arrangements that would make Jewish settlement in Transjordan feasible and permit joint development with Palestine, which the Jewish Agency could initiate and implement together with the Arabs of Transjordan. This would make it possible for Jewish settlement to be fostered and to improve the conditions of the inhabitants. . . . We have never excluded from our considerations those great, desolate, and uncultivated stretches of land across the river which are capable of settlement and development.[32]

And once again in March 1946, shortly before Britain terminated the mandate and recognized the independence of Transjordan, the Jewish Agency Executive objected to the Colonial Office that "the Jewish people had a contingent interest in the retention of Transjordan within the scope of the Mandate."[33]

On May 25, 1946, the emirate was transformed into the Hashemite Kingdom of Transjordan. The army of the new state, the Arab Legion, nonetheless remained under the control of Britain, which supplied, financed and provided the leadership for it. It was generally held that Transjordanian independence was a farce, since the country was so heavily dependent on British finance for its ordinary government operations. Indeed, when Transjordan applied for membership in the United Nations in July 1946, it was rejected. The United States refused to accord formal recognition to the country since its independent status was questionable. At the same time, Abdullah continued to press the Arab countries for agreement to his Greater Syria scheme. However, he was soon persuaded from a number of sources to announce on October 14, 1947, that he would not press his Greater Syria scheme any further until the Palestine problem was resolved.

Shortly thereafter, Abdullah held a secret meeting with Golda (Myerson) Meir, at the time head of the Political Department of the Jewish Agency for Palestine, at Naharayim in the Jordan Valley. It was clear that the British mandate over Palestine was coming to an end, and it was unlikely that the transition to independence would be peaceful. The rising tensions between the Arabs and the Jews, exacerbated by the basically irresponsible behavior of the British administration, seemed likely to make this a certainty. The question was, would there be peace or war between the forthcoming Jewish state and its Arab neighbors? Mrs. Meir wrote of the meeting:

> I came to Naharayim with one of our Arab experts—Eliahu Sasson. We drank the usual ceremonial cups of coffee, and then we began to talk. Abdullah was a small, very poised man with great charm. He soon made the heart of the matter clear: He would not join in any Arab attack on us. He would always remain our friend, he said, and like us, he wanted peace more than anything else. After all, we had a common foe, the Mufti of Jerusalem, Haj Amin el-Husseini. Not only that, but he suggested that we meet again, after the United Nations vote.
> On the way back to Tel Aviv, Ezra Danin, who had met with Abdullah often before, filled me in on the king's general concept of the role of the Jews. It was that Providence had scattered the Jews throughout the Western world in order that they might absorb European culture and bring it back to the Middle East with them, thus reviving the area. As for his reliability, Danin was dubious. It was not, he told me, that Abdullah was a liar, but that he was a Bedouin, and that the Bedouin had their own ideas about truth—which they saw as something much less absolute than we did. At any rate, he said, Abdullah was certainly sincere in his expressions of friendship, although they would not necessarily be at all binding on him.[34]

On November 29, 1947, the United Nations approved a partition plan for Palestine that called for separate Jewish and Arab states. The following month the Council of the Arab League vehemently rejected the plan and promised to defeat it. Nonetheless, on December 22, Abdullah announced that his Greater Syria plan offered the only viable solution to the Palestine problem. His own sense of confidence was undoubtedly bolstered by the fact that, as the British were preparing to withdraw from

Palestine and were refusing to cooperate in the implementation of partition, they were also anxious to reach a new understanding with Transjordan that would ensure the protection of their interests in the region. Negotiations on a new Anglo-Transjordanian treaty were scheduled to be held in London in March, only two months before the end of the mandate over Palestine and the withdrawal of British forces and administration. The British would certainly be amenable to the extension of Abdullah's realm to include the territory designated as the Arab part of an independent Palestine.

The delegation that came to London to negotiate the new treaty consisted of Premier Tawfiq Pasha Abul Huda, Foreign Minister Fawzi al-Mulqi, and Brigadier John Bagot Glubb, head of the Arab Legion. After the treaty discussions were completed, Abul Huda and Glubb met separately with British foreign minister Ernest Bevin on the question of the proposed Arab state in Palestine. Abul Huda suggested to Bevin that when the British withdrew, the Jews would immediately establish a state. However, the Arabs of Palestine were by no means as well organized and prepared as the Zionists to establish an Arab state. There was a danger, in his view, that such a vacuum might tempt the Zionists to disregard the boundaries proposed in the United Nations resolution and to occupy the territory assigned to the Arabs, perhaps as far as the Jordan River. Alternatively, the mufti of Jerusalem might seize the opportunity to assume control of the new Arab state. Neither possibility would serve the interests of either Britain or Transjordan. The best and easiest way to forestall both of these two possibilities would be to have the Arab Legion promptly occupy the areas assigned to the Arabs under the partition plan. At this point, Glubb interjected that it was impractical for the legion to occupy either the Gaza area or Upper Galilee. It would have to confine its area of control to the territory contiguous with Transjordan. Abul Huda agreed to such a restriction. Bevin's reply to this proposal was, "It seems the obvious thing to do, but do not go and invade the areas allotted to the Jews."[35] The collusion between Bevin and Abdullah thus aborted the birth of an independent Arab state in Palestine.

In the meantime, Abdullah continued to communicate with the Jewish leadership to whom he reiterated his assurances of nonbelligerency. At the same time, two developments took place which prevented the peaceful takeover of the West Bank as anticipated by Abdullah. First, the Palestinian Arabs attempted to close the road to Jerusalem, and Jewish forces moved into the Arab-designated area to keep the road open. Second, by the first week in May, 1948, it was clear that despite his assurances to the Jews, Abdullah had committed himself to joint action with the Arab League. Several days before the British mandate was due to expire, the Political Committee of the league convened in Amman to work out final arrangements for a coordinated effort in the forthcoming war. Abdullah tried to convince the assembled leaders that it was risky to go to war with the Jews, who were better prepared and organized. He argued that it might still be possible to reach a peaceful accommodation with them, but his colleagues would have none of it. They were determined to solve the problem by force, regardless of the risk. Abdullah met with Glubb immediately after the meeting. He told his commander: "If I were to drive into the desert and accost the first goatherd I saw, and consult him whether to make war on my enemies or not, he would say to me, 'How many have you got and how many have they?' Yet here are these learned politicians, all of them with university degrees, and when I say to them, 'The Jews are too strong—it is a mistake to make war,' they cannot understand the point. They make long speeches about rights."[36]

Having dispensed with the political aspects of the situation, the league leaders turned to the military. It was soon apparent that there was no real possibility of a coordinated effort. King Farouk would not consider submitting command of his Egyptian forces to anyone else, nor would Abdullah submit the Arab Legion, the only credible force of the lot and the underpinning of his regime, to foreign control. The only experienced soldier of any note was Glubb, the legion's commander, but the Arab leaders distrusted the British. Ultimately, it was decided that each belligerent would send a liaison officer to a joint operations center at Zarqa, near Amman.

At the same time, Glubb, pursuing the understandings reached in London, sent Colonel Desmond Goldie to meet with a representative of the Jewish defense force, Haganah, at Naharayim, across the Jordan. His mission was to try and reach an agreement with the Haganah that would relieve the Arab Legion of the need to fight in the war. Goldie proposed to Shlomo Shamir that the Arab Legion should occupy the Arab parts of the country, while both the legion and the Haganah would stay out of Jerusalem. The legion was prepared to wait two or three days before it crossed the border, to give the Haganah time to consolidate its control over the Jewish sectors of the country. Goldie was assured that if the legion did not attack Jerusalem, the Haganah would not do so either. As for Glubb's proposal, Shamir agreed to report it to his superiors.[37] Since neither Abdullah nor Glubb was in a position to control the other belligerents, the proposal must have struck the Zionist leadership as somewhat naive if not bizarre. Before long, Mrs. Meir requested another meeting with Abdullah to attempt once more to dissuade him from joining in the war. He agreed to meet, but insisted that she come to Amman, in secret of course.

With the fateful date only a few days away, Abdullah met with Golda Meir a second time on May 11, accompanied by Ezra Danin. Mrs. Meir reported the meeting as follows:

> Then Abdullah entered the room. He was very pale and seemed under great strain. Ezra interpreted for us, and we talked for about an hour. I started the conversation by coming to the point at once. "Have you broken your promise to me, after all?" I asked him.
>
> He didn't answer my question directly. Instead he said, "When I made that promise, I thought I was in control of my own destiny and could do what I thought right, but since then I have learned otherwise." Then he went on to say that before he had been alone, but now, "I am one of five," the other four, we gathered, being Egypt, Syria, Lebanon and Iraq. Still, he thought war could be averted. . . .
>
> So then I said to him, "You must know that if war is forced upon us, we will fight and we will win."
>
> He sighed and again said, "Yes, I know that. It is your duty to fight. But why don't you wait a few years? Drop your demands for free immigration. I will take over the whole country and you will be represented in my parliament. I will treat you very well, and there will be no war."[38]

Upon Mrs. Meir's return from the meeting, she handed David Ben-Gurion a note which stated: "I had a friendly meeting [with Abdullah]. He is very worried and looks terrible. He did not deny that we had agreed on a mutually satisfactory arrangement. According to his plan, this would mean a united country with autonomy for the Jewish section, and then, after a year, he would take over the Arab section. But now he is only one of five. It will be one country under his rule."[39]

Soon after this meeting, as noted by Alec Kirkbride, Abdullah was still anxious to reach some accommodation with the Zionists that would satisfy the other Arab states. He inquired if "the Jewish leaders would be prepared to cede to him some of the land allotted to them in the partition scheme, so as to persuade the Arab world to accept the division of Palestine." This sort of bargaining did not sit well with the Zionist leaders. Even the staunchest advocates of acceptance of the partition scheme were not happy with it. They agreed out of expediency, since it seemed to them the only way to get an international sanction for a Jewish state. However, appeasing the United Nations was one thing; appeasing the Arab states that had no legitimate interest in Palestine in the first place was out of the question. In fact, the Zionist leaders, most notably Ben-Gurion, had decided that if the partition scheme was not accepted by the Arabs as it stood, they would feel free to redivide the country as the opportunity presented itself. Accordingly, their response to Abdullah was "that the acceptance of the boundaries described in the plan approved by the United Nations Organization was subject to the partition scheme being implemented as a whole and in a peaceful fashion. If the Arabs went to war the Jews would retain anything they could win."[40]

Abdullah was apparently distressed by his own realization that events would not unfold as he had imagined. He had believed that if the partition plan were implemented, the other Arab states would first declaim loudly against it and then reluctantly, and under protest, accept it as a fact. Then, given his understanding with the British, he would add the territory envisioned for the Arab state in Palestine to his domain. For the most part, he was little concerned with precisely which tracts of territory were to become his as long as he would be able to expand the borders of his realm. As noted with bitterness by Nasir ad-Din al-Nashashibi of Jerusalem, who became his private secretary after the war, "Palestine was to King Abdallah nothing more than a piece of earth on which stood the al-Aqsa Mosque and, buried beside it, the remains of his father, King Husayn. That is all he saw in it. That was the limit of his understanding of it. . . . As to the homeland, the coastal plain, the wealth, the property and the cities—they did not interest King Abdallah at all."[41] He certainly did not consider those places as worth a risky conflict.

Abdullah's thinking was reflected by Glubb, the British commander of the Arab Legion, who observed that "when the Arab Legion originally planned to enter Palestine on the termination of the mandate, no war with the Jews had been visualized. It was proposed only to occupy the central and largest area of Palestine allotted to the Arabs in the 1947 partition. The Jews were most likely aware of this proposal and did not appear to object to it."[42] The Arab states had deluded themselves with an exaggerated sense of self-confidence. It was the Arabs of Palestine who had to pay for their folly. The only Arab leader of any consequence who understood the extent of the risk they were taking was Abdullah. He had consistently advised against overconfidence. He had the only military force of any real consequence which was commanded by experienced officers who understood the seriousness of the difficulties the Arab armies would face in the conflict. As Glubb later assessed what had happened, he explained: "One of the major causes of the Arab failure in 1948 was their unwillingness to face facts. Not only did they neglect to study the potential military strength of both sides, but they accused of treachery any man with a courage to speak the unpalatable truth."[43] Abdullah's own assessment was both more blunt and more profound: "My conclusion from all this is that the Arabs must give up daydreaming and apply themselves to realities."[44]

When the truce agreement brought an end to the fighting, only Transjordan emerged with substantial territorial gains. Egypt occupied the Gaza area, which was of strategic value but not much else. Abdullah was in control of almost all the territory allocated to the Arabs in the central part of the country. Perhaps most important, he had achieved control of the Old City of Jerusalem, which had great symbolic significance as well as political importance. Notwithstanding the general rejection of the unrealistic plan, of the United Nations mediator Count Bernadotte, which basically proposed that since everything was such a mess in the country the clock should be turned back and the partition scheme implemented once again, the British still attempted to retain the provision in it that called for the unification of Arab Palestine with Transjordan. As expected, on December 11, the General Assembly of the United Nations failed to adopt a resolution on Palestine supporting the plan. Abdullah, for his part, now had no recourse other than to take the practical steps necessary to ensure that the part of the projected Arab state that was under his military control would become part of his new and expanded kingdom.

It now seems quite clear that Britain, primarily in furtherance of its own interests in the region, did not want the Negev area to become part of Israel. It much preferred to see it incorporated within Transjordan for at least two reasons. First, it would provide a direct land bridge between Egypt and the rest of the Middle East, thereby ensuring territorial contiguity between all the members of the British-backed Arab League. Second, in the event of problems with Egypt, it would provide a suitable alternative location for the large British military infrastructure in the Suez Canal Zone. It was this latter consideration that probably most accounts for the strong British support of the Bernadotte plan. It also explains Britain's eagerness, at every opportunity, to charge Israel with violation of Transjordan's territorial integrity, presumably to justify British intervention and the dispatch of military forces to the territory in accordance with the provisions of the Anglo-Transjordanian Treaty. Nonetheless, after a number of unsuccessful attempts of this sort that were in clear violation of the truce, the British were embarrassed into halting their transparent support of Abdullah's attempt to seize the Negev. The Transjordan-Israel Armistice Agreement was finally concluded on April 3, 1949.

Abdullah derived two lessons from the conflict with Israel. It confirmed his original conviction that the Jews of Palestine were a potent force for progress in the region, and that he and the Arabs would have been better served had they reached a peaceful accommodation. It also validated his originally low estimate of the actual military capabilities of the Arab League states. But perhaps more important, in terms of Abdullah's primary interests, there could no longer be any doubt about the utter hostility of the Arab states to any extension of Hashemite power. This meant that if he retained any hopes of fulfilling his dream of a Greater Hashemite Syria, he would have to create it in spite of the universal Arab opposition to his goal. Nonetheless, he remained as committed as ever to proceed along what he now understood without a doubt to be a dangerous course.

5

From Transjordan to Jordan and Back

Abdullah's efforts to reach an amicable settlement of the Palestine problem in 1948 had fallen on deaf ears in the Arab capitals, and the failure to listen to him had proved disastrous for the Arab national movement. Not only was he rebuffed, his Arab allies had gone to lengths from the very outset to assure that Transjordan would reap no lasting benefit from the fact that it was the only Arab participant to come out of the conflict in control of a sizable tract of what was originally proposed as the Arab state in Palestine. As early as April 12, 1948, the Arab League passed a resolution precluding any of the Arab states that would send armies into Palestine from taking possession of any lands they might conquer. All such lands were to be turned over to the Palestinian Arabs. Abdullah's rejection of this proposition was reflected in Jordan's vote against the resolution.

With encouragement from the member states of the Arab League, an Arab Government of All Palestine, headquartered in Egyptian-occupied Gaza, was proclaimed on September 20, 1948, under the premiership of Ahmad Hilmi Pasha. A week later, Haj Amin al-Husseini, the mufti of Jerusalem, was elected president of an Arab Palestine National Assembly, also in Gaza, that claimed jurisdiction over all of Palestine. Within a month all the members of the Arab League, with the exception of Transjordan, extended formal recognition to the new regime of a Palestine it did not control. The obvious purpose of this charade was to prevent Abdullah from annexing those parts of Palestine under his control. It was believed that the mere existence of such a shadow indigenous Palestinian government would serve to constrain Abdullah's freedom of action. He could simply have ignored the All Palestine Government's existence, had he chosen to do so, since its writ covered only Gaza, and even there only to the extent that the Egyptians would permit it to exercise any authority. He elected instead to take more active, though cautious, steps to assert his authority in Palestine.

On October 1, 1948, some five thousand Palestinian Arab notables convened in Amman at a Palestine refugee conference at which they repudiated the mufti's government and, as might have been expected given the venue of the gathering, urged Abdullah to extend his protection over the country. Then on November 15, Adbullah paid a visit to the Coptic convent in Jerusalem's Old City. There the Coptic bishop crowned and proclaimed him "King of Jerusalem."[1] Next, on December 1, an Arab Congress of the national leaders of Arab Palestine under Transjordanian control convened in Jericho. The congress adopted a resolution which proposed that "Palestine and the Hashemite Kingdom of Transjordan be united into one Kingdom and that King Abdallah ben el-Hussein be proclaimed constitutional King over Palestine."[2] The resolution was promptly sent to the United Nations General Assembly and to the Arab League. It was then submitted to the Transjordanian cabinet, which approved it as the government's policy on December 7 and then presented it to the parliament in Amman, which gave its assent on December 13. It was expected that Abdullah would soon name himself king of Palestine.

Abdullah's opponents in the Arab world began to react in unproductive attempts to forestall what was to prove inevitable. King Farouk of Egypt sent a letter, dated December 13, to all Arab heads of state, rejecting the resolutions of the Jericho congress as unrepresentative of the majority of Palestinian Arabs and therefore invalid. The Arab League similarly attacked the resolution. Even the Council of Ulemas of al-Azhar University in Cairo denounced the prospective annexation of Palestine as "violating Islam's pledge to Allah."[3]

Abdullah responded to these challenges in kind, but not personally. To Farouk, Sheikh Muhammad Ali al-Jabari broadcast an open letter, reminding the Egyptian king of his utter failure to redeem his promise to liberate Palestine by force. Since he had failed, it would be better if he kept out of Palestinian affairs in the future. "Let us, the people of Palestine, save at least what is left of our country by peaceful means." To the ulemas of al-Azhar, Sheikh Suleiman Taji al Faruqi of the Palestine ulemas responded that what took place in Palestine was simply none of their business.[4]

In the meantime, the United Nations, apparently unconcerned by what was actually happening in Palestine, was busily engaged in pushing through a resolution calling for the internationalization of Jerusalem. This was part of the original partition resolution that had been vehemently opposed by all the Arab states. Now, however, these same Arab states became zealous supporters of internationalization, to deprive both Israel and Abdullah of their holds on the city. With regard to the latter, it was believed that without Jerusalem, and particularly the great mosques in the Old City, he might not be able to consolidate his control in Palestine. Thus, in October 1949 the Arab League Council adopted a resolution calling for the long-rejected internationalization of the city. This had the peculiar effect of making Transjordan and Israel allies in their joint opposition to the proposal. Commenting on the position of the Arab states in this matter at the United Nations, the Arabic newspaper of Jerusalem, *Falastin*, asked: "How can we adequately express our hatred for those Arab delegates at Lake Success who sacrificed Arab interests in Jerusalem for the sake of their political speculations and personal ambitions? It was the disunity and lack of public spirit on the part of those same Arab states that caused the loss of a large part of Palestine to the Jews a year ago. Now they want to be instrumental in losing the Mosque of Omar also."[5]

In face of the mounting opposition to his control of the West Bank, Abdullah began to move more decisively. He allowed the existing governorship of Palestine to lapse, and from December 16, 1949, on, all governmental affairs in the West Bank were conducted from Amman. On December 27 the Transjordanian parliament was dissolved and elections to a new parliament covering both Transjordan and Palestine were called for the following April. To assure stability on his meandering frontier with Israel as he moved to annex the West Bank, Abdullah proceeded to accelerate the secret negotiations with Israel on a security agreement. As noted by Walter Eytan,

> King Abdullah, alone of the Arab rulers, was sincere in regarding the armistice as a step toward peace. After the [armistice] agreement was signed, he sought a more permanent arrangement with Israel. Conversations with him and some of his closest advisers were carried on intensively, especially between November 1949 and March 1950. A draft treaty was prepared and initialed, but the King, under the rising pressure of an Arab extremism which scared his ministers, was unable in the end to carry it through. Desultory talks went on, but after a while it became clear that nothing could come of them, despite the personal efforts of the King and the concessions which Israel was ready to make.[6]

One of the major concessions offered by Israel was to grant Jordan an outlet to the Mediterranean by means of a corridor that would run across Israeli territory, connecting Jordan with the coast at Gaza. It would be Abdullah's responsibility to convince Egypt to turn Gaza over to him. As recorded by one of the participants in the discussions with Abdullah, Moshe Dayan:

> We pursued this idea and at one of our last meetings in Shuneh, on December 17, 1949, when I saw the king together with Reuven Shiloah, we reached the stage of drafting the terms of a peace treaty. The king was weary of the explicit term "peace treaty," but agreed to call it a "paper" on which were inscribed "Principles of a Territorial Arrangement (Final)." This "paper" was initialed by the king and Reuven Shiloah. I do not know whether the Israeli government would have ratified this agreement. Ben-Gurion did not reject it, but he wrinkled his nose when he read it. At all events, when we returned to the king to continue the negotiations, he informed us that his friend Sir Alec Kirkbride, Britain's minister to Transjordan, did not agree that Jordan should enter into such a treaty with Israel while other Arab states, mainly Egypt, had not done so. The king therefore asked us to regard the "paper" as cancelled.[7]

This outcome confirmed the judgment on the extent of Abdullah's freedom of action made by Ben-Gurion on December 18, 1948, when he told Moshe Dayan to go ahead and try to negotiate with the king. "Our future need is peace and friendship with the Arabs," he said. "Therefore I am in favor of talks with King Abdulla, although I doubt whether the British will let him make peace with us."[8]

The secret pact with Israel was supposed to remain in force for five years. It was intended to be an interim arrangement until a full peace treaty could be worked out. The armistice lines, with some minor adjustments, were to have remained in force without prejudicing the shape of the final agreement.[9] However, when word of the agreement eventually became known, the opponents of peace with Israel reacted with virulence. Prime Minister Abul Huda felt obligated to resign and stepped down on March 2, but was soon recalled when his replacement, Samir Pasha ar-Rifai, could not form a new government. Under the mounting pressure, including that provided from his influential British advisers, Abdullah quietly allowed the chance for peace with Israel to lapse. It appears that the British Foreign Office made the assessment that the advantages that Abdullah might reap from a normalization of relations with Israel were not commensurate with the risks involved for him and the Hashemite dynasty, and consequently for the security of Britain's own position in Transjordan.

The cessation of the peace initiative had virtually no impact on the anti-Hashemite campaign that had been set in motion. On March 19, the Cairo *al-Masri* proclaimed: "The time has come for the Arab League to cut off relations with Transjordan, a country that has betrayed Islam and Arab unity and the Arab cause. The time has come to sever this decayed member from the body of the Arab world and to bury it and heap dung thereon."[10] At its twelfth meeting, which opened a few days later, the Arab League took steps to block the no longer pending treaty with Israel as well as the annexation of the West Bank by Abdullah. On March 27, the All Palestine Government, now headquartered in Heliopolis, near Cairo, was invited to attend the meetings of the league's council. This led to a de facto boycott of the meetings by Transjordan, since it sent no delegation from Amman. However, it did permit its representative in Cairo to attend. The council reaffirmed its resolution of 1948 which precluded any Arab country from annexing any part of Palestine. The Transjordanian representative abstained from taking part in the vote.

A general election for the new Jordanian parliament was held on April 11, providing for equal representation from both the East and West banks. Eleven days later, Abdullah commented publicly on the Arab League's threat to expel Transjordan if it went ahead with annexation. "If expulsion comes as a result of unifying the two parts of this besieged nation," he said, "it will be welcome. We do not wish to be of those who oppose unity in the name of the Arab League, from which we had hoped good would come."[11] On April 24, 1950, at the inaugural session of the new parliament, Abdullah lashed out at the Arab League once again: "My Government considers the resolution adopted by the Political committee of the Arab League Council of April 12, 1948 as invalidated by the conclusion by the Arab states of a permanent truce and acceptance of the partition resolution, thereby contradicting the aforementioned . . . resolution." Later, in his memoirs, Abdullah gave vent to his personal feelings about the Palestine question: "It is apparent from the foregoing that in truth the Palestine problem is one of ignorance, obstinacy, and self-seeking on the part of persons who have throttled their homeland until they have almost completely destroyed its patriotic spirit. I bear witness to this before God and know that His anger will be mighty. But I am not of those who will be embarrassed before God and the tribunal of justice by any accusations against me."[12]

Both houses of the parliament, in joint session, then passed the following Resolution of Unity which was signed into law by Abdullah the same day: "Approval is granted to complete unity between the two banks of the Jordan, the eastern and the western, and their amalgamation, in one single state: the Hashemite Kingdom of the Jordan, under the crown of His Hashemite Majesty King Abdallah ben el-Hussein the Exalted. This will be upon the basis of parliamentary constitutional rule and complete equality in rights and duties of all the citizens."[13]

The opposition of the Arab League had proved ineffective against Abdullah's determination. Its council subsequently maintained that the annexation was illegal, but could not get the unanimity necessary to take effective action against Jordan. Finally, a face-saving formula was arrived at that Jordan was able to accept in the interest of maintaining the facade of unity in the Arab world. The Arab League thus passed a resolution on June 12, 1950, which declared that the annexation of the West Bank was simply a measure necessitated by immediate practical considerations, and was not intended to be permanent in character. It further stated that Jordan would simply hold the territory in question in trust until a final disposition of the Palestine problem was achieved, and that Jordan committed itself to accept, with regard to the future of Palestine, whatever might be decided unanimously by the other member states.[14]

Following Abdullah's annexation of the West Bank, his enemies in the Arab world began a virulent propaganda campaign against him. He was characterized as a British puppet and instrument of continued British control in the Middle East. Since the British were now being blamed for the Arab defeat in Palestine, notwithstanding Britain's repeated efforts to forestall the emergence of the Jewish state, the responsibility for the disaster was to be shared by Abdullah. Consequently, it became an imperative of Arab nationalism to get rid of both the British and their lackey Abdullah. As a result, the latter's relations with some of the Arab leaders on the West Bank became increasingly strained.

Abdullah was warned repeatedly that he was becoming a target for assassination by Palestinian extremists, but does not appear to have taken such warnings seriously enough. On Friday, July 20, 1951, as he was entering the al-Aqsa Mosque in the Old City of Jerusalem for services, he was shot to death. His death brought to an end his long-standing dream of a Greater Syria under Hashemite leadership. His successors would be preoccupied with trying to hold on to what he had achieved by expanding Hashemite rule to the West Bank.

After a year-long period of maneuvering over the succession to Abdullah, his eldest son, Talal, was dethroned on August 11, 1952, by a unanimous decision of both houses of the Jordanian parliament, which declared his minor son Hussein as king. A regency was established to govern the country until Hussein reached his majority.

At the time of Hussein's assumption of sovereign power in 1953, the Jordanian population of some two million was two-thirds Palestinian. One third consisted of refugees housed and fed by UNRWA, the United Nations refugee relief organization, in camps on both sides of the Jordan. Another third were West Bankers, who considered themselves to be Palestinians rather than Jordanians. Many of these tended to look upon Hussein and the Jordanians as alien usurpers of their patrimony, and were not reconciled to Amman's authority over their affairs. The remaining third were indigenous East Bankers, mostly Bedouins, who by now had developed a loyalty to the Hashemite dynasty. These demographic facts promised to create serious problems for any attempt to develop an integral Jordanian state under Hashemite rule. In 1954, the Jordanian parliament tried to mitigate the problem of the Palestinian majority in the country by passing a Nationality Law that granted Jordanian citizenship to anyone, except Jews, of Palestinian origin residing in Jordan. This offer was extended subsequently to all Palestinians living abroad who wished to acquire Jordanian citizenship, on February 4, 1960.

Before long, small unrelated groups of Palestinians from the refugee camps on the West Bank began making minor incursions into Israel across what was for the most part an open frontier. These actions gradually increased in number and severity until the Israelis began to consider them intolerable. Israel, of course, used its armed forces to retaliate. This was carried out by shelling and sometimes by direct assault on the Arab staging camps near the border. The character of these border incidents took on a new and more serious dimension in 1955. Egypt, anxious to assert its leadership of the Arab world, gave support and encouragement to groups of fedayeen who were encouraged to carry out terrorist acts in Israel. The Egyptian notion was that such terrorism, by its indiscriminate nature, would begin to undermine the country's apparently growing self-confidence. By 1956, the number and character of the fedayeen raids into Israel from Jordan began to provoke increasingly larger and stronger reprisal raids, taking an ever-larger number of lives, Jordanian as well as Palestinian.

As one consequence of the 1956 Sinai war between Egypt and Israel, which resulted in a second Egyptian defeat at Israel's hands, President Gamal Abdel Nasser decided to disband the Egyptian-sponsored fedayeen units. A continuation of such raids from Egyptian territory could produce Israeli reprisals, which Egypt was not ready to cope with in the wake of its recent defeat. Following Nasser's lead, the other Arab states that bordered Israel also decided to restrict fedayeen incursions from their territory to the extent that they could. The fedayeen idea, however, was well suited to the mood of frustration and despair that afflicted the youth of the Palestinian refugee camps. Even without external support, the desire to lash out at Israel spawned a number of clandestine Palestinian organizations committed to terrorist activity. They were, however, for the most part unstable and ineffective.

Nasser had become convinced by his experience of the Sinai war that it was unrealistic to predicate the achievement of his goal, that of building a vast unified state out of the diverse Arab countries, on the prior destruction of the Jewish state. Accordingly, he reversed his priorities. He would seek to achieve Arab unity first. The Arabs would then have the collective will as well as the means to eliminate the Jewish state in the Arab midst. On February 1, 1958, Nasser took the first major step toward this goal when Egypt and Syria became joined in the United Arab Republic. This was followed in March by the further unification of the United Arab Republic and the Yemen in an expanded confederation called the United Arab States. Nasser's next target was Hashemite Iraq, a country with a long record of instability. In Baghdad, a group of sympathetic officers began plotting the overthrow of the monarchy. At the same time, the regent, Abd al-Ilah, uncle of the underage king Feisal II, had ambitions of his own for Iraq. He had dreams of Hashemite dominance of an enlarged Arab state that would incorporate Syria, Jordan, Lebanon and Kuwait. As a first step toward his goal, formulated to some extent as a consequence of his opposition to Nasser's ambitions, Abd al-Ilah brought about a union between the two Hashemite kingdoms of Iraq and Jordan on February 14, 1958.

The Hashemite initiative was completely unacceptable to Nasser, notwithstanding his having sent a telegram of congratulations to Feisal, who emerged as the figurehead of the union, and steps were soon taken to rectify matters. The occasion was presented by the decision to send an Iraqi brigade to Jordan in the summer of 1958. The troops were led by Nasserist officers, who exploited the opportunity of their passing through Baghdad to join with another brigade already in the city and overthrow their own government. On July 14, 1958, Feisal was murdered along with his uncle, the regent, and the rest of the royal family. The prime minister, Nuri as-Said, met a similar fate. Thus ended the brief union of the Hashemite houses of Iraq and Jordan. Hussein appealed to Britain to help him preserve his rather shaky throne. Britain responded by airlifting troops across Israel, with the latter's clearance, to Hussein's aid. On January 17, 1960, Hussein accused the Arab leaders of dealing with the Palestine problem irresponsibly. He stated that "they have not looked into the future. They have no plan or approach. They have used the Palestine people for selfish political purposes. This is ridiculous, and I could say, even criminal."[15] In September 1960, Nasser's agents tried to finish his vendetta against the Hashemites by assassinating Hussein. A bomb was planted in the prime minister's office, set to explode at a time when the king was scheduled to be there. Hussein did not appear and the explosion killed only the prime minister.

Nasser had hoped to unite the Arab world, regardless of the cost. However, his achievements in this regard proved to have little permanence. In 1961, a coup in Damascus brought an end to Syria's participation in the United Arab Republic. This meant, in effect, that the United Arab States was dismantled as well. Yemen thus became free of Egypt. However, when Ahmad, the king of Yemen, died in 1962, a group of Nasserist army officers, with Egyptian backing, seized power and proclaimed a republic. This coup brought Egypt into a proxy conflict with Saudi Arabia, which continued to support the royalists. Egypt became directly embroiled in a five-year struggle that sapped its strength, contributing significantly to Nasser's ultimate abandonment of his pan-Arab dreams.

By 1963, frustrated by the failure of his attempts at unification of the Arab states, Nasser was seeking new vehicles for bringing the Arab states together under his leadership. The Palestinian cause appeared to him to offer one means of progress toward that elusive goal. The humiliation of the Arab defeat by the Jews was shared by all the Arab states in common, and they had all exploited the Palestinian cause for their domestic political purposes. It could thus also be made to serve as a focus for rallying the diverse elements of the Arab world around the Egyptian president's leadership. For this purpose, Nasser had need of an indigenous Palestinian organizaton that could presume to represent the Arabs of Palestine, one that could be given inter-Arab legitimacy by the Arab League while actually remaining under his control. To set this scheme in motion, Nasser used the occasion of a summit meeting of Arab heads of state that he convened in Cairo in January 13–17, 1964.

The reason for the meeting was to discuss the Arab reaction to Israel's completion of its project to divert the headwaters of the Jordan River. The Arabs had consistently refused to accept any Israeli plan for diversion of waters to meet its needs, and had long threatened to block any such attempt with force. Now that the Israeli project was nearing completion, their repeated threats to use force to stop it, especially by Syria, became a matter of deep concern to Nasser. It was clear that if there were to be an attempt by Syria to stop the Israeli project, it would necessarily involve both Egypt and Jordan, neither of which was in any position to go to war with Israel. Half of Egypt's army was bogged down in Yemen, with no relief in sight. For Jordan, the risk was especially great since a defeat could cost Hussein the West Bank and probably his throne as well. Nasser's primary interest at the summit meeting was therefore to get the various Arab governments to agree not to go to war against Israel at that time, making them share the moral responsibility of inaction in the face of what they had consistently characterized as Israeli aggression, and to put pressure on Syria not to take unilateral action that could drag Egypt into a premature conflict.

Since the assembled heads of state had agreed to do nothing about Palestine, it was necessary to take some step that would demonsrate that they had not swept the issue under the rug. The establishment of the Palestine Liberation Organization served that purpose very nicely. The PLO would present a visible reminder of the commitment of the Arab states to the liberation of Palestine and the return of the Palestinian refugees to their homes. At the same time, it was not expected to do anything that could embarrass the Arab states or provoke Israel into taking action against them. In other words, the purpose of the PLO, as far as Nasser and most of the other leaders were concerned, was to make noise but do nothing. Nonetheless, as the primary sponsor of the PLO, the Egyptian president could proclaim his leadership of the universal Arab nationalist cause, effectively forcing the other Arab leaders to acknowledge his preeminence.

As Nasser had anticipated, the establishment of the Palestine Liberation Organization was approved by the summit conference. The assembled leaders then committed themselves to the organization's support, and voted an appropriation of funds for its operating budget. Nasser's choice for the presidency of the PLO, Ahmad Shuqairy, was approved as well. Shuqairy's appointment was intended to ensure that the PLO would be ineffectual. He was an aging Palestinian diplomat who had previously served as Saudi ambassador to the United Nations, and was well known in Arab diplomatic circles as an opportunist and charlatan. The previous September, Shuqairy had been invited to represent Palestine at the Arab League, notwithstanding the objections raised by Hussein, who had sound reasons for his opposition to Shuqairy's appointment to the league as well as to the creation of the PLO. Most of the Palestinians to be represented at the Arab League lived in Jordan, and had been given Jordanian citizenship. This meant that their interests should have been represented at the league by Jordan. Consequently, the granting of a separate Palestinian representation to the league reflected an implicit challenge to the legitimacy of Jordan's rule over the West Bank. Hussein had no illusions about Nasser's reasons for bringing the PLO into being. Hashemite Jordan would clearly be the first target of Nasser's new vehicle for bringing the Arab states into his embrace. To obtain Hussein's agreement to the establishment of the PLO, which was essential for Nasser's purposes, the Jordanian king was given an undefined promise that the PLO's freedom of action would be constrained.

The inaugural conference of the Palestine National Council, the governing body of the PLO, was held in Jerusalem during May and June 1964. Hussein, as host head of state, had little choice but to give it his blessing. He made it clear, however, that he did not want any PLO operations to be mounted from his territory. On June 1, 1964, the PLO issued its first declaration, which set the organization's goal as the liberation of Palestine. The Palestinian National Covenant declared Palestine to be an Arab homeland, and further stipulated that Arab unity and the liberation of Palestine were two complementary aims. The incorporation of Arab unity in the covenant as an aim equal to that of liberation clearly reflected Nasser's viewpoint. As an accommodation to the concerns of the frontline Arab states regarding possible future PLO claims, the 1964 covenant specified, in Article 24, that "this organization does not exercise any regional sovereignty over the Western Bank in the Hashimite Kingdom of Jordan, on the Gaza Strip or the Himmah Area."[16]

The PLO was authorized to establish a military arm, the Palestine Liberation Army (PLA), and small units were formed and armed on conventional lines in both Egypt and Syria. Shuqairy had hoped to trigger a revolution by the Arabs inside Israel. To help promote this goal, Shuqairy planned to establish PLO bases in the West Bank near the Israeli border, where he expected to have more freedom of action than in either Egypt or Syria. However, he soon found himself in open conflict with Hussein, who would neither allow PLA units to occupy positions along the Israel-Jordan frontier nor permit Shuqairy to levy taxes on the Palestinians in the refugee camps. To bolster security along the sensitive frontier with Israel, Hussein in 1965 disbanded his part-time 30,000-man National Guard, which was responsible for border security, because it was composed primarily of West Bank Palestinians who were now no longer considered to be reliable. The guard was replaced by contingents of regular Jordanian army forces.

In the meantime, the Baathist party which took power in Syria by a coup in 1963 was disinclined to allow Nasser to continue as the preeminent sponsor of the Palestinian cause. Not very different from Nasser in ideology and ambition, the Baathists had visions of a united Arab nation under Syrian hegemony, the first step toward which would be a Greater Syria. The Palestinian cause could be used to serve their purposes just as Nasser was exploiting it to serve his. Accordingly, shortly after the PLO came into being in 1964, the Syrians began to develop their own

Palestinian resistance organization. Colonel Ahmad Sweidani, head of Syrian intelligence, set his agents to work in the refugee camps in Lebanon where they recruited Palestinians to be trained as fedayeen. One of the Syrian agents in Beirut was approached by a small group called the Movement for the Liberation of Palestine, or Fatah. The group was originally founded in 1959 and had begun to grow when the announcement of the Egyptian-sponsored and Arab League–backed PLO brought about the defection of most of its members. In addition, Algeria, which had been supporting the group and had allowed training camps to be set up there, withdrew its financial support which it then transferred to the PLO. They were thus floundering when they came into contact with the Syrian agent. The Fatah approach to dealing with the Palestine problem was well received by the Syrians. The plan was as simple as it was bold. It was also the reverse of Nasser's strategy. The Egyptian leader believed that Arab unity had to be achieved before the major battle with Israel. Fatah's strategy was predicated on the idea that it was the battle itself that would forge Arab unity. Fatah proposed to carry out an ongoing series of increasingly outrageous terrorist acts inside Israel that would provoke the Israelis into massive retaliations; in response, the Arab states would be forced to cooperate in a new war with Israel that would result in the destruction of the Jewish state.[17]

Concerned about the threat posed by the Egyptian-backed PLO to his regime, Hussein saw the emergence of Fatah as a means of countering Nasser's attempts to unseat him. Thus, by giving de facto permission for Fatah to operate out of Jordan, Hussein could hope to build support for himself among the Palestinians by demonstrating that his opposition to the PLO was not based on any reluctance on his part to address the Palestine issue, especially since he was well aware that Fatah's program would precipitate Israeli reprisals in Jordan. However, he did not believe that such actions would threaten his regime as much as those of Nasser and the PLO. It was a gamble he was prepared to take. Accordingly, with Syrian backing and Jordan's tacit complicity, Fatah personnel began to cross into Israel from Jordan (not Syria). While bemoaning Fatah's illicit use of Jordanian territory, Hussein did little to prevent it. Furthermore, and notwithsanding ostensible objections from Jordan's government, fedayeen camps were set up at Jenin and Qalqilya near the Israeli border. To mitigate the severity of the anticipated Israeli reaction, Hussein secretly sent a message to the Israeli government disclaiming any responsibility for fedayeen raids originating from Jordanian territory. Israel was initially responsive to Hussein's disclaimer and cooperated in his sporadic and highly visible campaigns to gain control over the fedayeen. From time to time, lists of Jordanians collaborating with Fatah were provided to Amman by Israeli intelligence, accounting for massive arrests by the government.[18] Those arrested were for the most part promptly released. Fatah's planned campaign to provoke Israel into massive reprisals began on the night of January 15, 1965, when it attempted to interrupt Israel's national water grid. Throughout the year, at least another twenty-six raids were mounted from Jordanian territory. As Fatah wished and planned, Israeli reprisal attacks on the fedayeen bases in Jordan began, and soon exceeded Hussein's expectations. His strategy was beginning to backfire. In October 1965, Hussein told the Jordanian parliament that he would not support the use of Jordan as a base for Palestinian fedayeen groups. "Such organizations will give Israel an excuse to attack our people before we can adequately defend ourselves."[19]

Jordan, however, was now not only under assault from Israel. As a consequence of the Syrian-backed fedayeen raids, it was also under growing pressure from the Egyptian-backed PLO, which sought to bring down the Hashemite regime. In a sense, Jordan rather than Israel was becoming the primary Palestinian and Arab target. Hussein's relations with Shuqairy and the PLO took a dramatic turn for the worse in April 1966, when the government shut down the PLO headquarters in Amman because of its subversive activities and arrested numerous PLO personnel. Hussein now became virtually the exclusive target of the PLO propaganda machine. Notwithstanding the self-imposed restrictions of its own covenant, the PLO began publicly to challenge the very legitimacy of Jordan as an independent state. As Hussein put it, "They had begun to practice subversion on a grand scale. They were trying to divide the populations of the east and west banks of the Jordan. They were taking into their ranks people who belonged to what we considered illegal political parties, such as the Baathists, Communists, and leftist nationalists. Actually, their goal was to replace Jordan's monarchy with some other political authority."[20] By July 1966, the government of Jordan broke off its relations with the PLO. Hussein took the occasion to begin to move against the Fatah as well, even though the relations between Fatah and the PLO at the time were inconsequential. However, because of the popularity of the fedayeen in Jordan, Hussein had to treat them solicitously. In the fall of that year, Fatah carried out a series of actions near Jerusalem which provoked a major Israeli reprisal attack near Samu on November 13, during which the Jordanian army suffered numerous casualties. This event triggered a number of violent anti-Hussein demonstrations in the West Bank, demanding action from the Jordanian government against the Israelis. A state of emergency was declared. The Council of the Arab League met in extraordinary session in Cairo, where Shuqairy proposed that the Kingdom of Jordan be transformed into a Palestinian republic. On November 25, in a broadcast from Cairo, the PLO demanded the immediate resignation of all ministers in Jordan's government who were of Palestinian origin and called upon the police to support the anti-Hussein demonstrations. The Fatah strategy appeared to be working. The crisis in Jordan had demonstrated Fatah's capacity to force events in a direction of its choosing.

Notwithstanding the mounting tension with Israel, Jordan rather than Israel remained Nasser's primary target, with the PLO serving as his chosen instrument. The Israeli attack on Samu was seized by Shuqairy as the basis for renewing his demands for the organization of a PLO army to protect the West Bank. Egypt, Syria and Iraq lent their support to the PLO demand and, going even further, called for the stationing of the unified forces of the Arab states in Jordan. Because of Hussein's refusal to meet these demands, he was accused by Nasser of being ready to sell out the Arab nation to the Israelis. Syria went so far as to call for the overthrow of the Hashemite regime.

Hussein struck back as best he could. On January 3, 1967, he closed the PLO offices in Jerusalem, forcing the organization to relocate its headquarters to Cairo. Jordan then withdrew the official recognition granted to the PLO at the 1964 Arab summit meeting on the grounds that its main objective had become not the liberation of Palestine but the overthrow of the Jordanian government. The PLO had become, in Amman's view, nothing more than an extension of Egypt's intelligence services. The acrimony between Cairo and Amman reached a new high and Jordan decided to recall its ambassador.

Egypt and Syria, in receipt of substantial arsenals of Soviet weapons, were now emboldened by Moscow to become more directly provocative toward Israel. The two Arab countries signed a mutual defense pact in March 1967. The continuing Fatah raids across the border, calculated to bring about Israeli reprisals, placed increasingly heavy political pressure on Nasser to take some action in support of the Palestinian initiative. Egged on by the Soviet Union, Nasser started on a course of risk taking that soon got out of hand. Jordan, for its part, helped push Egypt along a path that was destined to lead to disaster, although not intentionally. In self-defense against the broad-ranging propaganda attacks against Hussein coming from Egypt, Jordan wanted to give Nasser a bit of his own medicine, by demonstrating to the Arab world that Nasser could not be taken seriously by anyone, especially not the Israelis. On May 16, Radio Amman challenged, "If the Egyptians really mean what they say, let them demonstrate their real intentions by expelling the UN force."[21] The implication of the taunt was that as long as the United Nations Emergency Force (UNEF), that had separated Egyptian and Israeli forces along the frontier since 1957, was still in place, Nasser could always use its blocking presence as an excuse for inaction. Nasser called for the removal of the UN force from the Israeli frontier the very next day. On May 18, U Thant, secretary-general of the United Nations, agreed to evacuate UN forces from the demilitarized zone at Gaza. Hussein later stated, "This surprising move on the part of the U. N. Secretary-General was unprecedented. I was now convinced that a military confrontation with Israel was inevitable."[22] Jordan's armed forces were placed on alert. Notwithstanding Hussein's alleged concerns about a war with Israel, the Jordanians continued to goad Egypt. On May 19, Radio Amman raised the question as to whether Egypt would in fact close the Straits of Tiran, between the Red Sea and the Gulf of Aqaba, since Israeli ships were still passing through them. As though to call Nasser's bluff, it argued in its broadcast, "Logic, wisdom and nationalism make it incumbent on Egypt to do so, because closure of the Gulf of Aqaba to Israeli navigation will destroy the Negev reconstruction plan and prevent the immigration of millions of Jews to Israel."[23] On May 23, Nasser announced the blockade of the international waterway through the Straits of Tiran, notwithstanding the UN resolution of March 1957 which had guaranteed freedom of transit through its waters. The Egyptian president should certainly have understood that this choking off of Israel's only direct maritime access to the Indian Ocean was an act of war that Israel could not ignore. In any event, Hussein, by his own admission, believed war to be inescapable. He stated, "I was convinced that it was no longer possible to pull back or to put out the smoldering fire."[24] Hussein may thus have served as the provocateur that pushed Nasser past the point of no return on the road to war.

Hussein's intentions during this crisis appear muddled. On the one hand, he had good reason to be concerned about the popular resentment against him in the West Bank. If he remained out of the coming war as he had done in 1956, that resentment might boil up into open rebellion. His cousin, Zeid bin Shaker, a brigade commander at the time, later suggested that there would have been civil war if Hussein had not joined Nasser in the challenge to Israel.[25] Hussein's own apologia elevated his decision to a higher plane: he later claimed that he was morally obligated to enter the war because he was a signatory to the Arab Defense Pact of 1964 and could not stand aside while the other Arabs fought. It seems equally likely that Hussein acted impulsively and capriciously, if not irresponsibly.

Jordan, which had anticipated the escalation of the crisis, had begun to mobilize its forces on May 18, the day that U Thant responded to Nasser's request for the removal of UN forces from Sinai, and was in a full state of readiness by the twenty-fourth. Convinced that once war broke out Jordan would be a prime Israeli target, Hussein sent his army chief of staff, General Amer Khammash, to Cairo to find out what Egypt's war plans were. Khammash returned on May 28 with the disconcerting news that the United Arab Command, called for in the defense pact, was defunct. As far as the Egyptians were concerned, the current crisis with Israel was a bilateral matter between them and the Syrians. In effect, the affair was none of Jordan's business. Hussein had been snubbed by Nasser. The very next day, Hussein was persuaded by his senior military advisers that it was essential from a security perspective to end Jordan's isolation in the Arab world in the event of a new full-scale war between the Arab states and Israel. Hussein was forced to swallow his pride. He summoned the Egyptian ambassador and told him that he wanted to see Nasser as soon as possible. Nasser's invitation came late at night on the twenth-ninth. Shortly after dawn on May 30, Hussein flew to Cairo.

After some discussion with Nasser, Hussein proposed that Egypt and Jordan sign a defense pact modeled on that between Egypt and Syria. Nasser, however, insisted that it was essential that Hussein reconcile himself to the PLO first, and then invited Ahmad Shuqairy to join them as the new defense pact was endorsed. Nasser took the occasion to force Hussein to swallow another bitter pill. He asked him to demonstrate his solidarity with the PLO by taking Shuqairy back to Jordan with him in his own aircraft.[26]

Nasser's plan of attack called for Syrian, Iraqi and Saudi Arabian troops, under a unified command, to move into and take up positions in Jordan. This deployment would then be followed by a coordinated simultaneous assault on Israel from the south, east and north. Jordan's decision to join with Egypt and Syria made war virtually inevitable. For Israel, the threat was no longer just the question of the closure of the straits. The prospect of combined Arab armies in Jordan posed a serious threat to the very existence of the state. Hussein thus played a highly significant role in precipitating the conflict that was about to take place.

Shortly after the outbreak of hostilities in the south, Israel's prime minister, Levi Eshkol, broadcast a message which stated that "we will not attack any country which did not first launch an attack against us. But any aggressor can be sure of being met by the full might of the Israeli arms."[27] Israel clearly did not want Jordan to enter the war. Hussein had avoided doing so in 1956, and Israel saw no real justification for his doing so now. Jordanian forces began shelling the Jewish part of Jerusalem at 8:30 A.M. on June 5. The Israelis did not respond in kind. Instead, still hoping that the war could be localized, Prime Minister Eshkol sent an urgent message to Hussein through three separate channels: General Odd Bull, the head of the United Nations Truce Supervision Organization in Jerusalem; the Israeli representative on the Israel-Jordan Mixed Armistice Commission, who passed it on to his Jordanian counterpart; and the United States Embassy in Tel Aviv. The message was unequivocal: "We shall not initiate any action whatever against Jordan. However, should Jordan open hostilities, we shall react with all our might and he [Hussein] will have to bear the full responsibility for all the consequences."[28] One Western ambassador was present when Hussein decided to reject Israel's overture for peace. The king told him that he had to join the conflict because he had just been assured by Nasser that the Egyptian army was marching on Tel Aviv and that the Egyptian air force could provide him with the necessary air cover to protect his forces against an Israeli counterattack.[29] According to Hussein, when he received General Bull's message by telephone, he responded to Eshkol's appeal by saying, "They started the battle. Well, they are receiving our reply by air."[30] What Hussein did not know when he made this arrogant response was that the squadrons of aircraft sighted heading north from Egypt to Israel were not Egyptian planes en route to attack Israel. They were Israeli aircraft returning from their destruction of the Egyptian air force on the ground that morning.

The Jordanian army had six infantry brigades deployed on the West Bank, in addition to two armored brigades. There were additional forces in readiness on the East Bank. All Jordanian forces had been placed under the command of General Abdel Moneim Riad, an Egyptian, who had just arrived to direct the combined Arab forces on the Jordanian front. On June 5, the first day of the war, the Israelis tended to provide considerable leeway to the Jordanians. It was not yet entirely clear to them that the latter could not be induced to stay out of the conflict. When it became evident later that day that Israel was in fact at war with Jordan, it promptly attacked and destroyed Hussein's small air force. The promised Arab reinforcements never arrived. There was no offensive battle plan other than a general notion of driving a wedge through Israel to the Mediterranean to divide the country in two. And there was no defensive plan at all. When Jordan found itself under attack rather than on the offensive, confusion reigned supreme.

On the second day the Israelis made a series of probes along the entire length of the front, searching for positions that would be vulnerable to deep penetration thrusts. Without air cover, Jordan's armored brigades were soon smashed. The Israelis penetrated the defenses of Jerusalem and fought their way through the sector north of the Old City to reach the Augusta Victoria Ridge, which dominates the area. By that evening Riad had already concluded that it was a lost cause and recommended that Hussein ask for a ceasefire and withdraw his remaining forces to the East Bank. Hussein refused to yield even though he later admitted that "at 2 P.M. on Tuesday, June 6, the situation was perfectly clear. For me, this so-called war was lost."[31] Nevertheless, most of the forces defending the Old City withdrew under cover of darkness that same night, leaving behind only a handful of snipers.

On the third day, Wednesday, June 7, the Israelis took the Old City and Jericho, and penetrated to the Jordan River during the afternoon. They now had effective control of the entire West Bank. When Hussein forwarded a message that morning to the Israeli defense minister, Moshe Dayan, requesting a negotiated ceasefire, Dayan responded: "We have been offering the King an opportunity to cut his losses ever since Monday morning. Now we have 500 dead and wounded in Jerusalem. So, tell him that from now on, I'll talk to him only with the gunsights of our tanks."[32] Jordan, over a period of three days, had been transformed in everything but name and institutions back into Transjordan. As Jordan's prime minister Wasfi al-Tal later put it: "We could easily have avoided this premature war. Of course, we hardly expected such a devastating defeat. But with the information we had, we didn't believe in the possibility of victory either."[33] What Abdullah had gained through shrewdness was squandered by Hussein through foolishness.

6

Hussein, the Palestinians and Israel

Hussein's foolhardiness had cost him dearly. However, for reasons that are difficult to fathom, he managed to create the impression abroad that he was an unwilling victim of circumstances beyond his immediate control, a stance he would continue to adopt successfully for the next two decades. Thus, in early 1968, when United Nations special representative Gunnar Jarring was engaged in trying to arrange negotiations between the belligerents on the basis of UN Resolution 242, an urgent message from President Lyndon Johnson was brought to Israeli prime minister Levi Eshkol by the American ambassador. In it the president suggested that Hussein was prepared to negotiate with Israel on the basis of Resolution 242, but his situation was precarious. Israel was urged to be understanding of the king's predicament and therefore to be forthcoming with additional concessions that would make it possible for him to move toward peace. The Israeli prime minister's immediate response to Ambassador Walworth Barbour was recorded by Gideon Rafael:

> Eshkol replied that Hussein's situation had been precarious from the beginning of his reign and would remain so until its end—hopefully a happy one. Israel had always been understanding and had pleaded with

Hussein at the outbreak of the hostilities with Egypt not to participate in the war. He had dismissed Israel's appeal and that was the only reason for his present distress. He compared the King's plea now with that notorious defendant who had murdered his father and mother and begged mercy because he was a poor orphan.[1]

It was certainly true that Hussein's situation had always been precarious and was even more so now. Before the June 1967 war, about two-thirds of the population of Jordan had been Palestinians. Hussein was well aware that he was widely regarded as an alien intruder imposed on the country by the British. His ability to maintain his control of the country depended primarily on the loyalty of his Bedouin allies. Like his grandfather Abdullah, he was neither particularly well liked nor trusted. It was common knowledge that Abdullah had used the Arab Legion to help the British suppress the Palestinian Arab rebellion in the late 1930s, and in 1948 he had appeared quite content to salvage for himself what he could out of the West Bank. Hussein thus inherited the challenge of forging a coherent Jordanian nation out of an essentially apathetic if not hostile population that felt little if any loyalty to the Hashemite house. The emergence of the Palestine Liberation Organization made this task far more difficult, and ultimately perhaps impossible.

When the PLO was founded in 1964, and the Palestinian National Covenant formulated, it stipulated the territory to which the name Palestine applied as follows: "Palestine, with the boundaries it had during the British Mandate, is an indivisible territorial unit." Since Transjordan was created and administered under the British mandate until it was given independence in 1946, the geographic extent of the Palestine contemplated by the PLO quickly became an issue of vital import for Jordan. When the covenant was drafted, Hussein was assured that the PLO considered only the area west of the Jordan River to be Palestine. However, since Jordan had annexed the West Bank, PLO activities there as well as on the East Bank were viewed with some apprehension. Jordan had extended its citizenship to the Palestinian Arabs in 1954, including both those who were on the West Bank and those who had relocated to the East Bank. The covenant's assertion that "Palestine is the homeland of the Arab

Palestinian people . . . and the Palestinian people are an integral part of the Arab nation" threatened to undermine Amman's efforts to create a unified Jordanian state out of the East and West banks. Furthermore, it was hardly accidental that the 1968 revision of the covenant dropped the article of the 1964 version that placed the West Bank and Gaza outside the scope of the PLO's claims of sovereignty. Since Hussein had lost the West Bank, as far as the PLO was concerned, he also forfeited any legitimate claim to sovereignty there. The PLO thus signaled Hussein that the West Bank would become part of a new Palestinian state and would not revert to Jordanian control. Furthermore, to offset the possibility of Israel reaching an accommodation with the indigenous West Bank leaders to establish an independent entity under an Israeli security umbrella, the Palestine National Council adopted a resolution on July 18, 1968, declaring its "categorical rejection of the idea of establishing a spurious Palestinian entity in the territory of Palestine occupied since June 5, and of any form of international protection. The Assembly hereby declares, moreover, that any individual or party, Palestinian Arab or non-Palestinian, who advocates or supports the creation of such a subservient entity is the enemy of the Palestinian Arab people and the Arab nation."[2] By precluding the acceptability of a Palestinian state in the West Bank, Palestinian aims could only be realized in Cisjordan as a whole, or in Palestine as it was understood before 1921, that is, a Palestine composed of both Cisjordan and Transjordan. Hussein's worst fears about the aims of the PLO were becoming realized.

The idea that Palestine and Jordan were intrinsically one and the same was argued by the Egyptian writer Ahmad Baha ad-Din in 1968. He wrote:

> A state called Palestine must thus from now on serve as our fundamental starting point. Such a state will regroup Jordan, on both banks of the Jordan river, and Gaza; that is to say it will consist of all that remains of Palestine plus what used to be called Transjordan and was, before that, a part of Palestine. . . . The restoration of the name "Palestine" will have an immense moral and political effect in the world during the next stages of the conflict. When the old original name of the country has been revived,

it will be clear that there is a Palestinian state, part of which has been annexed, a state which demands legal redress for that annexation.[3]

Such a state could then serve as the base for a new and ultimately successful onslaught against Israel. Such a view, of course, was the very antithesis to Hussein's goal of incorporating Palestine within Hashemite Jordan. Furthermore, it made no provision for Hussein or his royal successors. It was virtually inconceivable that he could be accepted as king of a Hashemite Palestine.

With the loss of the West Bank, including East Jerusalem, Hussein had no choice but to return to Transjordan and begin the difficult and laborious process of restoring confidence in his regime and consolidating his grip on what he had salvaged from the humiliating defeat. It was true, at least in terms of territory, that Nasser's loss was far greater than his. However, the desert of Sinai had never been an integral component of the Egyptian state, and Gaza had never been annexed and incorporated in the country. But for Hussein, the war had been an unmitigated disaster. He had lost the West Bank, which contained about half his population, and with it the very rationale for the Kingdom of the Jordan. The loss of Jerusalem was particularly galling as its possession symbolized the continuing centrality of the Hashemites within the Arab and Muslim worlds. What he needed most now was a respite that would allow him to reconstitute his severely reduced realm. Instead, within a few months he had to contend with a new challenge that threatened the very stability of the country. The reemergence of the fedayeen movement, now constituted in a number of reasonably well-structured organizations, proved to be very popular. The fedayeen alone could afford to spout continued defiance of the enemy without being subjected to ridicule. They had not sued for peace, nor breathed a sigh of relief that the Israelis had not crossed the Jordan and occupied parts of the East Bank. Their posturing provided a vicarious release for the frustration of the masses in face of the disaster they were led into by the Arab governments.

Since Jordan now provided the only front in proximity to the heart of Israel, the fedayeen descended on Jordan in droves, ostensibly for the purpose of conducting guerrilla operations against Israel. It seems quite clear that Hussein could have prevented or contained this influx had he so desired. However, at the time, it was in Hussein's interest to encourage instability in the West Bank to prevent the Israelis from coming to an accommodation with the local leaders that might result in an independent Palestinian state there not under his control. Indeed, Aziz Shihadeh has called attention to the secret document published in the Jerusalem Arabic daily *al-Quds* on September 27, 1970. "According to this document, the Government of Bahajat al-Talhouni asked the American Secretary of State through the Jordanian Ambassador in Washington in October 1967 to bring pressure to bear on Israel and make her desist from her policy of supporting the establishment of a Palestinian State, threatening that 'should Israel persist in her intentions, Jordan would be compelled to abrogate all agreements, secret and not secret, relating to Israel.' "[4]

Shortly after the June 1967 war, there was in fact a proposal being pushed by highly respected Israelis, such as Mattityahu Peled, that called for an independent Palestinian state in the West Bank that would in effect be an Israeli protectorate. Under this proposal, Israel would be responsible for the security of the state. Peled pointed out that, contrary to the view that such an arrangement would prejudice the sovereignty of the Palestinian state, such arrangements were in fact far from unusual in the contemporary world. "At present most European states operate within a framework of similar treaties which enable their confederates to maintain armed forces within their sovereign territory. This is true on both sides of the Iron Curtain. . . . In general, such arrangements bear witness to a special identity of interests and to a particularly close relationship between the states who maintain these interests."[5]

While this position seemed to offer a theoretically valid way out of the West Bank dilemma, it never really represented a politically viable option for Israel. It was, however, sufficiently threatening to generate common concern, albeit for different reasons, among Yasser Arafat and the fedayeen and Hussein. Thus there emerged a covert Jordanian complicity in the growth and activity of the fedayeen, while the government in Amman publicly bewailed its inability to prevent the country from turning into a fedayeen base.

Some of the fedayeen units were trained in Egypt and, along with members of Palestinian units in the Egyptian army, were sent to Jordan, where they came under the supervision of the military attaché at the Egyptian embassy in Amman.[6] The largest fedayeen base in Jordan was at Karameh in the Jordan Valley, north of the Dead Sea. It quickly became the communications center and headquarters for Fatah and other groups, and was the operational base from which most fedayeen assaults across the border took place. On March 18, 1968, an Israeli school bus struck a fedayeen-laid mine on a road near the Jordanian border south of the Dead Sea. Three days later, two Israeli armored forces supported by paratroops swept across the border to encircle and wipe out the Karameh base. The action inevitably engaged the Jordanian army, which could not be certain of Israeli intentions notwithstanding the leaflets that were dropped explaining that the attack was aimed solely at the fedayeen base. It soon developed into a pitched battle, with considerable casualties among both Israelis and Jordanians. The Karameh base was demolished and close to two hundred fedayeen were killed. Arafat and an aide escaped on motorcycles and fled to Salt, about sixteen miles to the east.

Salt, a town of some 30,000 residents and located beyond the range of Israeli artillery, now became the chief fedayeen base from which most of the subsequent incursions into Israel and the West Bank were made. In August 1968, Israel retaliated for the increased number of fedayeen attacks with a destructive air raid on the installations at Salt. Hussein went to the town shortly after the attack and offered to visit the nearby fedayeen installations that had been badly damaged. To his chagrin, the fedayeen refused to allow him to enter. Their general arrogance and blatant disregard of Jordanian law caused Hussein at one point to instruct the army to surround three of their bases and order them to leave within forty-eight hours or be removed by force. The fedayeen refused to budge and the army, instead of attacking them, withdrew, causing the government considerable embarrassment. After the attack on Salt, most of the fedayeen bases were relocated to the Palestinian refugee camps, where it was believed they would be less prone to Israeli retaliation.

Before long, the fedayeen were to be found swaggering around the streets of Amman and other population centers fully armed.

There were repeated incidents of their interference with the Jordanian security forces. In general, the fedayeen conducted themselves like an ill-disciplined army of occupation, rather than as guests in the country. They established their own revolutionary court system outside the framework of Jordanian law. Prisoners who had been abducted by them from the West Bank, and were found guilty in the fedayeen courts of spying or collaborating with the enemy, were sentenced to death and executed. The fedayeen freely financed some of their expenses by extortion at gunpoint from shopkeepers, businessmen and foreign residents in the capital. They had, in effect, created a state within a state. The government of Jordan found itself in a virtual power-sharing arrangement with the fedayeen, who were being directly supported by a number of foreign Arab governments.

The fedayeen presence soon became intolerable, as they posed an increasing threat to the stability of the Jordanian state, which was being transformed into a Hashemite-fedayeen condominium. Hussein could ill afford to allow the situation to continue indefinitely. The fedayeen clearly challenged his ability to rule the country effectively. At the same time, he could not afford to take effective action against them because of their popularity among the large number of Palestinians in Jordan. Indeed, at one point, Jordan set up its own fedayeen organization, the Front of National Sacrifice, under Hussein's uncle, Sherif Nasser bin Gamil. It was disbanded, however, after having made several forays against Israel.[7]

For a time, all Hussein could do was wait for the right moment to move against the fedayeen groups. That moment appeared to come in the wake of the street demonstrations in Amman in November 1968 that marked the fifty-first anniversary of the Balfour Declaration. One of the small groups of demonstrators stoned the American Embassy. The rioters were quickly dispersed by the Jordanian police, and a number of fedayeen leaders were arrested. The government then sent troops to take control of the headquarters of the group that had attacked the embassy. The headquarters, of course, was located in a refugee camp. The fedayeen resisted the attempt of the Jordanian force to take over their installation. Their efforts received the backing of the refugees, resulting ultimately in the death of several dozen people.[8] It seemed that Hussein had misjudged the extent of the popular support of the fedayeen, and could not prosecute the matter further without risking a civil war. He felt compelled to appeal to President Nasser of Egypt to intervene with the fedayeen on his behalf.

An agreement between the government of Jordan and the fedayeen was then worked out and signed. It outlawed the wearing of fedayeen uniforms and the carrying of arms in populated areas. It prohibited the fedayeen from establishing roadblocks and stopping and searching vehicles. It stipulated that they would have to cooperate with the state security forces and be subject to the state judicial system. Superficially, the agreement brought the fedayeen under the law of the land. At the same time, however, the agreement also served to validate the existence of an independent political entity within the state. It authorized the fedayeen groups to issue their own identity cards to their members. It allowed them to exercise certain police powers in cooperation with the state authorities. It also provided for a coordinating committee, representative of all the groups and the government, to be established in Amman. The committee was to mediate any disputes that arose between the fedayeen organizations and the state. The fedayeen thus emerged from their confrontation with the Jordanian government stronger than ever, and soon disregarded the constraints on their freedom of action ostensibly required by the Egyptian-brokered agreement.

In 1968, the fedayeen groups took over control of the Palestine Liberation Organization. When the fourth Palestine National Council met in Cairo in July 1968, it fundamentally changed the constitutional structure of the PLO. Whereas the organization's membership had previously consisted of individual Palestinian notables and others committed to the struggle against Israel, it was now transformed into a body of representatives of the various fedayeen and other Palestinian organizations. The Palestinian National Covenant was revised, under the dominating influence of Yasser Arafat's Fatah, to avow that the goal of the destruction of the Zionist state was to be achieved only through armed struggle. In a sense, the PLO was for the first time in its history freed from domination by foreign Arab powers, including Egypt, that could not foreswear the possibility of using political means to bring about victory for the Arab cause without incurring unacceptable diplomatic liabilities in the international arena. In February 1969, at the fifth PNC meeting in Cairo, Arafat was elected chairman of the PLO. Within a year, all the remaining fedayeen groups of any significance had come under the PLO umbrella.

The threat to Hussein's regime from the fedayeen continued to increase. Hussein remained ambivalent, however, with regard to how to deal with them. In addition to the domestic popularity of the terrorist attacks against Israel, there was also the fact that the same countries that were the main sources of finance for the fedayeen, Kuwait and Libya, also contributed a substantial portion of Jordan's annual budget. An open clash with their clients would engender the risk of isolating Jordan both politically and economically. Hussein appealed to the fedayeen groups to exercise more restraint, but his overtures went unheeded. On February 10, the Jordanian minister of the interior, Rasoul Kilani, issued an order which again banned the carrying of weapons in Jordanian towns and required the registration of all motor vehicles with the authorities. This was seen by the fedayeen as a frontal challenge to their autonomy, and they decided to resist the order. Clashes between them and the Jordanian security forces began to occur. It quickly became clear to the government that it would require a major armed and violent confrontation to bring the fedayeen under effective control. Hussein decided that the risks were too great at the moment. Instead, he suspended the order in return for a commitment from the fedayeen leaders to place their men under greater control and discipline. It was a clear political victory for the fedayeen, since it was obvious that Hussein was compelled to retreat from an open confrontation with them.

On May 6, 1970, reflecting its growing strength and self-confidence, the PLO succeeded in getting all its factions to agree, for the first time, to the statement that "the Palestinian struggle is based on the belief that the people in the Palestinian-Jordanian theatre are one people, that the people of Palestine are part of the Arab nation and that the territory of Palestine is part of Arab territory."[9] This somewhat ambiguously worded statement suggested the possibility of a renewed challenge to the legitimacy of the Hashemite state. The notion of a "Palestinian-Jordanian theatre" could imply a unified state on the East and West banks under Palestinian rather than Hashemite rule. The issuance of this statement was followed by an attempted assassination of Hussein in June. This precipitated a thirty-six-hour clash between the Jordanian army and the fedayeen. Once again, however, Hussein apparently felt that the time was not yet ripe for a serious confrontation with the PLO. For the moment, he was content with restoring a semblance of order in the country.

The announcement of the Rogers Plan in June 1970 finally provided the opportunity that Hussein had long awaited. The plan raised the possibility that under American pressure the Israelis might be forced to retreat from the West Bank as they had been compelled to withdraw from Sinai after the 1956 war. On July 26, Hussein announced Jordan's acceptance of the American peace initiative. As a result, a significant portion of the Palestinian population in Jordan began to dissociate itself from the fedayeen, who were now viewed as spoilers after the PLO rejected the plan. The Palestinian refugees from the West Bank were more concerned with the possibility of returning home across the Jordan than they were with Arafat's demands for the liberation of all of Palestine. With the prestige of the PLO at a low point, it having lost the allegiance of many Palestinians, Hussein concluded that his long-awaited opportunity was at hand. All he needed was the necessary provocation to justify an all-out assault on the fedayeen.

Sensitive to the increasing loss of popular support, during the summer of 1970 the fedayeen escalated their efforts to weaken Hussein. In a sense, the capacity to become the preeminent voice in Palestinian affairs, as well as their very position in Jordan, depended on their ability to convice the masses that they and not the king were in real control of the country. If this could be established, Hussein would forfeit the ability to speak for the Palestinians at the proposed peace talks, and the Rogers Plan would fail to achieve the expected breakthrough. It was clear to Hussein that the Rogers Plan might be his only chance to regain the West Bank and Jerusalem, as well as to make a permanent breach between the Palestinians and the fedayeen groups, which were beginning to pose a serious threat to continued Hashemite rule in Jordan. Hussein's concerns could only have been further heightened by the public position taken by some Israelis that was directly supportive of the overthrow of Hashemite Jordan and its

Hussein, the Palestinians and Israel

transformation into a Palestinian state. Proponents of this view argued that such an event would serve to relieve the deep frustration of the Palestinians; while not satisfying their maximalist demands, it would nonetheless force them into a position where they would be less willing and ready to take steps that ran great risks of losing what was now tangibly theirs. Thus, as argued by Shlomo Avineri in 1970, "one of the paradoxes of Arab society is that only radicals can afford to be moderate, whereas moderates tend to play to the radical gallery. . . . If the guerrillas became the government in Jordan, it would be difficult for them, even if they received Soviet support, to escalate their military activity beyond the present level. For they would then have to take into account the price the population in the Jordan Valley is paying for their activities—a consideration which they now dump in Hussein's lap."[10]

Hussein began to assert his authority over the fedayeen groups by attempting first to restrict their freedom of movement and action. Arafat reacted by mounting a violent propaganda campaign against the king, effectively calling for the overthrow of the regime. To further complicate matters, the fedayeen continued launching raids into Israel from Jordan that provoked Israeli reprisals, further demonstrating Hussein's lack of control of the country. At the end of August 1970, there were a number of open clashes between the fedayeen and Jordan's security forces. On September 1, there was another unsuccessful attempt to assassinate Hussein.

Then, on September 6, 1970, four international airliners were hijacked by members of the Popular Front for the Liberation of Palestine. Two of the aircraft, one American and the other Swiss, were flown to a desert airstrip near Zarqa, north of Amman. For three days some four hundred passengers and crew were held hostage. On the ninth of the month, another hijacked British plane was brought to the desert airstrip. The hostages were gradually released, and then the three aircraft were blown up. This latest outrage, coupled with at least two recent assassination attempts against him by radical Palestinians, spurred Hussein to decide that he could wait no longer.

Hussein's civilian government, however, was hesitant to mount the necessary campaign against the fedayeen. Accordingly, on September 16, Hussein dismissed the civilian cabinet and replaced it with one made up of twelve generals under the premiership of Muhammad Daoud. On September 17, Hussein's trustworthy Bedouin troops attacked the fedayeen bases and headquarters in the refugee camps. The assault developed into a major battle that raged for eleven days. Numbers of Palestinians in the Jordanian army defected and joined the fedayeen. These were later incorporated within the Palestine Liberation Army as the Yarmuk Brigade.

A number of Arab states appealed to Hussein to stop the fighting, hoping to gain a respite for the beleaguered fedayeen. Syrian commandos crossed the frontier on September 18 and attacked the villages of Et Turra and Shajara, intending to relieve the fedayeen by drawing Jordanian attention away from them to the northern border. Then, early on September 20, a Syrian armored force of some three hundred tanks painted with the insignia of the Palestine Liberation Army crossed the border into Jordan and began rolling south toward Amman. Before the day was through, the Syrian column had taken Irbid and threatened to reach Amman the following day. That same evening, Hussein instructed his close confidant, Zaid Rifai, to appeal to the American ambassador for urgent outside intervention "from any quarter" to stop the Syrian advance. National Security Adviser Henry Kissinger immediately contacted the Israeli ambassador in Washington, General Yitzhak Rabin, and urged Israel to take action to halt the Syrians. Kissinger told him: "King Hussein has approached us, describing the situation of his forces, and asked us to transmit his request that your air force attack the Syrians in northern Jordan."[11] The Israelis, however, were reluctant to make such a move without an assurance from Washington that the United States would undertake to prevent Soviet interference. Furthermore, Israel wanted a clear assurance of American support in the event that fighting broke out again on the Egyptian front. While the negotiations with Washington were underway, Israel redeployed two armored brigades to battle positions directly opposite Irbid, in plain sight of the Syrians.[12] Hussein, encouraged by the Israeli move and the movement of units of the U. S. Sixth Fleet closer to the Syrian and Lebanese coasts, felt confident enough to send his own forces north to engage the Syrians. It was clear to Damascus that Israel would not long accept the Syrian intervention in Jordan. The strong possibility of an Israeli counterintervention convinced the Syrian commander, General Hafez Assad, not to attempt to use his forces in further support of the PLO. The Syrian columns turned back toward their own border and abandoned the fedayeen to Hussein. Instead, Assad took advantage of the military mobilization to overthrow the Syrian regime in a bloodless coup. On September 25, Kissinger called Rabin once again to convey a personal message to his prime minister from President Nixon: "The president will never forget Israel's role in preventing the deterioration in Jordan and in blocking the attempt to overturn the regime there."[13]

On September 27, Nasser convened a meeting of Arab heads of state in Cairo. It was to be a meeting of reconciliation that Hussein could not refuse to attend. Nasser would not give up until he successfully got Hussein and Arafat to shake hands and reach an agreement on a modus vivendi. The accord called for the qualified toleration of PLO forces in the cities of Jordan, but neither Hussein nor Arafat was committed to making it work. It was too late for a compromise solution. The accord was out of step with the realities of the situation in Jordan, and was not to last very long. No sooner had the last of the assembled dignitaries departed from Cairo than the Egyptian leader suffered a fatal heart attack. With Nasser gone, Hussein promptly repudiated the agreement and proceeded with the liquidation of the fedayeen presence in Jordan.

The PLO break with Jordan now appeared irreversible. Accordingly, the eighth Palestinian National Council meeting (February 28–March 4, 1971) declared, in effect, that Jordan was and had always been Palestine:

> Jordan is linked to Palestine by a national relationship and a national unity forged by history and culture from the earliest times. The creation of one political entity in Transjordan and another in Palestine would have no basis either in legality or as to the elements universally accepted as fundamental to a political entity. It would be a continuation of the operation of fragmentation by which colonialism shattered the unity of our Arab nation and the unity of our Arab homeland after the First World War. . . .

> In raising the slogan of the liberation of Palestine . . . it was not the intention of the Palestine revolution to separate the east of the River from the west, nor did it believe that the struggle of the Palestinian people can be separated from the struggle of the masses in Jordan.[14]

The struggle with the fedayeen now developed into a full-scale civil war that lasted until July 1971. By the time Hussein was through, most of the fedayeen had either been arrested or ejected from the country. Hussein's actions against the fedayeen earned him the almost universal condemnation of the Arab world and the bitter enmity of Syria. The PLO organizational infrastructure was relocated to Lebanon.

On March 15, 1972, Hussein issued his own plan for a federal kingdom that would "guarantee the reorganization of the Jordanian-Palestinian house in a manner which will provide it with more intrinsic power and ability to work to attain its ambitions and aspirations." The proposed new structure would be a United Arab Kingdom which would "consist of two regions: (a) The Palestine region which will consist of the West Bank and any other Palestinian territories which are liberated and whose inhabitants desire to join it. (b) The Jordan region which will consist of the East Bank." The following day, Israel's prime minister Golda Meir reacted to the plan by reminding Hussein that he was "treating as his own property territories which are not his and are not under his control."[15]

Hussein's plan also provoked a strong reaction from Arafat, who rallied Fatah and the other PLO factions to oppose it. A hard anti-Hashemite stand was adopted at the tenth Palestine National Council held in 1972. The PLO now considered Jordan to be a major obstacle to the liberation of Palestine. Jordan's right to an independent existence was called into question. The PLO was unequivocal in its opposition to a Hashemite Jordan, and sought a united front of the Palestinian and Jordanian people to establish "a democratic state on Palestinian and Jordanian soil to assure the national sovereignty of both peoples."[16]

In its political program, announced in Cairo on January 12, 1973, the Palestine National Council adopted a "programme of action in the Jordanian theatre" which included a need "to struggle to achieve freedom for the Palestinian revolution to act in and from Jordan and to establish its bases in Jordanian territory, and to expose the conspiracies of the subservient regime and its misrepresentations in this connection, and to ensure protection by the masses of combatants who operate from and return to the territory west of the river."[17]

On September 12, President Anwar Sadat convened a tripartite summit meeting in Cairo to plan for the coming conflict with Israel. It seemed almost like a replay of 1967. Hussein had to think long and hard about joining Egypt and Syria this time. He had entered the 1967 war precipitately and paid dearly for his poor judgment. When the October 1973 war broke out, Hussein mobilized his forces along the length of the Jordan front. This time, however, he procrastinated, and in the end stayed out of the conflict. His prudence further reduced his stature among the other Arab states. The Arab League Summit Conference in Algiers issued a secret resolution in December 1973 that called for a "commitment to restoration of the national rights of the Palestinian people, according to the decisions of the Palestine Liberation Organization, as the sole representative of the Palestinian nation."[18] Understandably, Jordan "expressed reservations" about the resolution. It was clear that the Arab states were going to put Hussein in his place by publicly subordinating Jordan's vital interests to those of the PLO.

In the meantime, confidential exchanges of views with Israel continued. At one point, Israel proposed the reinstatement of Jordanian administrative control over the West Bank, while it continued to be responsible for security matters. It was prepared to leave the question of sovereignty open. Another time, it indicated readiness to grant Jordanian sovereignty over the Muslim holy places in Jerusalem and to evacuate the heavily Arab-populated sections of the West Bank. Israel insisted, however, on retaining the Jordan River as its first line of defense. Hussein would not agree to any of the Israeli proposals. It was not that he was unwilling to regain control of the West Bank in stages, he wanted Israel to withdraw entirely from the Jordan Valley, something Israel would not consider for security reasons.[19] He was later to lament repeatedly that his prudence in not getting involved in the 1973 war with Israel gained him nothing whereas the belligerents, Egypt and Syria, both regained some of the territories they lost in the 1967 war.

Hussein's intransigence over coming to any agreement with Israel that did not essentially restore the entire West Bank and East Jerusalem to him ultimately caused the Israelis to lose interest in dealing with him at all. Nevertheless, many senior Israeli officials continued to believe that at some point they could reach an agreement with him that would bring the peace between the two countries that, according to the popular myth, his grandfather Abdullah had hoped to realize. In the eyes of others, however, his outrageous demands for the restoration of the status quo ante were so far out of touch with geopolitical realities that he personally had become an impediment to peace, and should be treated accordingly. As Moshe Dayan put it, Hussein

> permits himself the luxury of viewing reality in fanciful terms when he proposes plans for a settlement of the problems with Israel. He ignores the fact that for almost twenty years Jordan denied Jews access to the Western Wall in Jerusalem, contrary to the stipulation in the 1949 Armistice Agreement; that in 1967 he joined in the war against us even though Nasser had not asked him to and Prime Minister Eshkol had warned him against doing so; that even after that war he permitted the terrorists to use his territory as a base of operations against Israel; and that some of his army units cooperated with them. In spite of all these realities, Hussein still believed that Israel should return to the pre-1967 borders, and rely on Jordan's word that if she did so, it would mark the opening of a new chapter: the Arabs would unreservedly respect the integrity and rights of Israel.[20]

In 1974, the twelfth Palestine National Council adopted resolutions that formally reflected its now official antipathy toward Jordan. The meeting issued a resolution calling for the establishment of an independent national fighting authority. It was made clear, however, that the independent fighting authority was intended to be a first step in a prolonged struggle against both Israel and Jordan. The goal of this struggle was to realize the establishment of a Palestinian-governed democratic state in all of Palestine. The resolution stated that the PLO would "struggle along with the Jordanian-Palestinian National Front, whose aim will be to set up in Jordan a democratic national authority in close contact with the Palestinian entity that is established through the struggle."[21] Whatever ambiguity was deliberately inserted into this statement regarding the future of Jordan from a PLO perspective, was completely absent from Arafat's position as expressed in a letter to the Jordanian Student Congress in 1974. Arafat asserted, "Jordan is ours, Palestine is ours and we shall build our national entity on the whole of this land after having freed it of both the Zionist presence and the reactionary-traitor [Hussein] presence."[22]

That same year, Hussein found himself completely isolated at the Seventh Arab Summit Conference in Rabat. Shortly before the meeting took place, Hussein had visited Sadat and, at the conclusion of their talks, the two issued a joint communiqué which specifically acknowledged Hussein's right to negotiate the future of the West Bank. At the summit, however, Sadat abandoned Hussein and joined in affirming "the right of the Palestinian people to establish an independent national authority under the command of the Palestine Liberation Organization, the sole legitimate representative of the Palestinian people in any Palestinian territory that is liberated."[23] Notwithstanding Hussein's nominal public adherence to the Rabat Conference resolution of October 29, 1974, he refused to take any measures that would strengthen Arafat's political or military credibility. Thus the king did not permit the PLO to reestablish its bases in Jordan, or carry out attacks on Israel from Jordanian territory. An ongoing power struggle ensued between Hussein and Arafat over control of the Palestinians in Jordan and the West Bank. Jordan continued unilaterally to subsidize various Palestinian institutions in the West Bank, while Arafat relied on the use of terror there to maintain the political position of the PLO.

Hussein told Moshe Dayan, during their meeting in 1977, "We Arabs will never agree to a territorial compromise. Have you ever asked yourself what such a compromise means from the Arab standpoint? It means to recognize the legality of the conquest of part of the territories which you seized from us and to this we cannot agree."[24]

Notwithstanding Jordan's rejection of the Camp David agreements of 1978, and its refusal to participate in the autonomy talks called for in the accords, Hussein never excluded the possibility of negotiations based on his federation plan of March 1972. Hussein and other Jordanian spokesmen continued to maintain that

Jordan's federation plan provided the only viable peaceful solution to the Palestinian problem. His opposition to the Camp David accords was strictly pragmatic. If there was a principle involved, it was simply that Jordan would not agree to any solution of the problem that did not assure Hussein's domination of the West Bank. The notion of an independent Palestinian entity there was completely anathema to him. He made this very clear during a meeting with President Jimmy Carter on January 1, 1978. As far as Hussein was concerned, "The people of the West Bank–Gaza should have the right to self-determination but not the right to claim independence."[25]

Jordan consistently argued in favor of this limited concept of Palestinian rights to self-determination in an unrelenting effort to achieve acceptance of Hussein's 1972 federation plan. It specifically and repeatedly rejected the notion that self-determination implies sovereignty. According to the Jordanian information minister Adnan Abu-Awda, "Self-determination means possession by the Palestinians of the freedoms and rights specified by the Human Rights Charter. These freedoms encompass the social, cultural, and economic rights necessary for free political self-expression."[26] The federation plan was seen as the appropriate instrument for guaranteeing those rights. Former Jordanian prime minister Abd al-Hamid Sharaf expressed a similar view: "The Palestinians and the Jordanians do not belong to separate nationalities. We have not forsaken our rights in the West Bank."[27] Notwithstanding the official Jordanian stance, Yasser Arafat sought to build a working relationship with Hussein. Arafat saw such collaboration as a useful tactic in advancing the cause of Palestinian self-determination and sovereignty in the region encompassing both banks of the Jordan.

With the appointment of Ariel Sharon as Israel's minister of defense in 1981, Israel accelerated its efforts to develop an indigenous anti-PLO leadership in the West Bank. It based its endeavor on the fact that the majority of the West Bank population was rural in character and primarily concerned with the problems of daily living, whereas the bases of PLO support were to be found among the lumpenproletariat, intellectuals and students in the urban areas. Consequently, the Village Leagues, first established in the Hebron region in 1979, became the focus of Israeli overtures. It was hoped that political and material support for the Village Leagues would help weaken the PLO's grip on the population of the West Bank. It was also well known that some of the key leaders of the leagues were prepared to contest the PLO's claim to be the sole representative of the Palestinian Arabs. Some had gone so far as to indicate their interest in negotiating a political settlement with Israel.

The Village Leagues, however, posed a threat not only to Arafat's legitimacy but to Hussein's as well. In the face of this new challenge, the two agreed to collaborate in thwarting the efforts of the leagues to become partners to the autonomy talks under the Camp David umbrella. The leaders of the Village Leagues were characterized as self-seeking traitors to the Palestinian cause and collaborators with the enemy. A Jordanian government edict issued by the prosecutor-general on March 9, 1982, proscribed membership or activity in the Village Leagues as high treason under Jordanian law and therefore subject to a penalty of death and confiscation of property.[28]

In September 1982, President Ronald Reagan proposed a new peace initiative to resolve the Arab-Israel conflict. The Reagan Plan was in essence a slightly revised version of the 1970 Rogers Plan. It called for the establishment of a self-governing Palestinian entity to be located in the West Bank and Gaza Strip, that was to be linked to Jordan in some form of association. This idea also came very close to Jordan's 1972 federation plan. The fundamental similarity between the two plans was unmistakable, and the Reagan initiative quickly received Hussein's support. Jordan called upon the PLO and the Arab states to back it as well. The PLO, of course, understood that the Reagan Plan denied the PLO any effective role in the Palestinian future, and rejected it as unacceptable. A statement issued by the PLO's Central Council, a sixty-member consultative group, denounced the Reagan Plan for ignoring "the right of our people to self-determination and to establish its own independent state under the leadership of the PLO, without which there can be no lasting peace in the Middle East."[29]

Unimpressed by the PLO's stance, the United States began to focus its diplomatic efforts in the Middle East on Jordan. This U.S. position seemed to leave the PLO out in the cold unless they were prepared to enter the peace process under the Jordanian umbrella, since their direct participation was rejected by both the United States and Israel. Arafat, however, made the astute judgment that as long as the Arab world remained faithful to its official stand of recognizing the Palestinian right to an independent state, Hussein's ability to take effective part in negotiations based on the Reagan Plan was severely limited.

The political aftermath of the war in Lebanon appeared to corroborate Arafat's assessment. The Arab summit at Fez, September 6–8, 1982, rejected the Reagan Plan's concept of a self-governing Palestinian entity in the West Bank and Gaza linked to Jordan. Instead, the Fez resolutions emphasized the Palestinians' right to a state of their own under the leadership of the PLO. Hussein, as was to be expected, seemed to go along with the Fez summit decisions. This gave further credence to Arafat's judgment regarding how far Hussein would be willing to step out of the bounds of an Arab consensus that rejected the Reagan Plan and with it Hussein's own federation plan. In interviews with the Western media, Hussein, perhaps biting his tongue, characterized the Fez resolutions as "a major milestone in the annals of the Arab world."[30] Hussein went so far as to invite Arafat to join him in discussions regarding the future relations between Jordan and the PLO, within the framework of a peace agreement within the context of the Fez resolutions. It was soon clear, however, that there was little probability of Hussein making any concessions on the crucial issue of Palestinian sovereignty. The king continued to press his original federation plan under the guise of a Palestinian state in the West Bank and Gaza in confederation with Jordan. He insisted on the establishment of the proposed confederation in a way that effectively precluded the eventual emergence of an independent Palestinian state; that is, the confederation was to be set up prior to the establishment of the Palestinian entity in the West Bank and Gaza. In effect, this meant that when the West Bank was handed over by Israel it would immediately come under Hussein's control. Arafat, on the other hand, was equally determined that confederation should follow the establishment of the Palestinian state, to ensure PLO control of the West Bank and Gaza.

Hussein's total opposition to the very idea of an independent Palestinian state also determined the Jordanian position regarding Palestinian representation in any negotiations. Arafat, wishing to capitalize on anti-Hashemite sentiment in the Arab world, called for a joint Arab delegation to the peace negotiations that would include not only PLO and Jordanian representatives, but those of other Arab states as well. Given the stance taken by the Arab states at Fez, Hussein would not countenance negotiating Jordan's vital interests while Arab states without a real stake in the peace process sat at the same table, constraining his freedom of action. At a meeting with Jordanian leaders in early 1983, Hussein observed that future ties between Jordan and the Palestinians were "a matter for the two sides only. No one else must be allowed to interfere in the forging of these ties or the weakening of them, be he Arab or foreigner, from the east or the west."[31] Hussein would brook no outside interference with his tactic of agreeing in principle to Palestinian demands for self-determination and a state of their own, while in practice taking precautionary measures to ensure that such a development would never take place. Considering the long-standing and conflicting motives and aspirations of Hussein and Arafat, there could be little question that any real Jordanian concessions to the PLO on the matter of Palestinian sovereignty in the West Bank would contribute to undermining Amman's ability to maintain control over the Palestinian population of the East Bank. Indeed, the acceptance even of the principle of Palestinian sovereignty could place the continued existence of the Hashemite dynasty itself in jeopardy. Hussein's carefully worded statement of July 31, 1988, ostensibly disavowing any further Jordanian interest in the West Bank, must be assessed in the light of these realities, which continue to prevail.

Afterword

In considering the future of the West Bank, there appear to be at least four basic possibilities, each of which may have a number of variations. The first is the retention and ultimate annexation and absorption of the territory by Israel. The second is the establishment of an independent Palestinian Arab state in at least those parts of the West Bank that are heavily populated by Arabs. Third, there is what has become known as the Jordan Option, that is, reaching an accommodation between Jerusalem and Amman that would turn most of the West Bank back to Jordan. Finally, there is the alternative of maintaining the status quo for an indefinite period.

With regard to the first, there is strong sentiment among a substantial number of Israelis for retaining permanent control over the regions of Judea and Samaria (West Bank), the very heart of traditional and historical ancient Israel. It was primarily the internal debate in Israel over the question of how to absorb the large number of Arabs there into the Israeli polity, without altering its predominantly Jewish characteristics, that prevented the Likud-led coalition governments of Menachem Begin and Yitzhak Shamir from pressing for its annexation, as was done in the case of the Golan Heights. The current inability to resolve

Afterword

this difficult and delicate issue has led to an internal political impasse that continues to divide the country.

The argument in favor of retention and ultimate annexation is fundamentally nationalist in character. The regions of Judea and Samaria were historically the heartlands of ancient Israel and were always considered by all Zionists, regardless of political orientation, as essential components of the state they aspired to recreate in the Jewish homeland. Even though these regions were excluded from the area assigned to Israel under the UN partition scheme of 1947, Zionist claims of a right to these territories were not nullified by the acceptance of partition as a practical measure deemed necessary at the time. In any event, the Arab refusal to accept partition, followed by Abdullah's illicit occupation and annexation of the West Bank and subsequent loss by Hussein of Judea and Samaria to Israel in 1967, has created a new reality. From a nationalist perspective, it would be unconscionable to relinquish the territories, which are integral components of Israel's patrimony, although for reasons of expedience, a government of Israel might not choose to exercise its inherent rights there. Thus, Prime Minister Begin's position was that Judea and Samaria must come under Israeli control and become a vital part of Eretz Israel. However, in acknowledgment of the serious unresolved problems of absorbing the Arabs of the territories into Israel, Begin proposed, as an interim measure, the temporary preservation of the status quo, which avoided the sensitive issue of sovereignty. This was the basis of the autonomy plan proposed by Begin that became part of the Camp David accords with Egypt.

According to Arye Naor, Israel's cabinet secretary under the Begin government (1977–1982),

> Menachem Begin did not conceive of and articulate the autonomy plan, nor did his government approve it, in order to sever Judea and Samaria from Israel or to bring about the establishment of a Palestinian state or to transfer the territories to any foreign sovereignty. Begin's autonomy plan was designed to evade the problem of sovereignty. The very idea of autonomy already constitutes a serious ideological and practical concession; but there cannot be an Israeli renunciation of its full right to

sovereignty in *Eretz Israel* even if that right is not exercised due to political considerations.[1]

The arguments against annexation are essentially twofold. First, there is the problem of demographics. Since the Arab birthrate in present-day Israel and the West Bank is substantially higher than the Jewish birthrate, and assuming only limited emigration, annexation of the West Bank will ensure an Arab majority in Israel within the next several generations. This will of necessity change the fundamental character of the state. The fulfillment of the Zionist aspiration for a Jewish National Home requires an independent national state in which there is a substantial Jewish majority, rather than a multinational state in which the Jews are again a minority.

Discussing the implications of attempting to absorb the West Bank, Yehoshafat Harkabi has pointed out,

> If we grant all the Arabs political rights as Israeli citizens, then they will constitute a near majority or majority in the Knesset. The first thing they will do is demand equality as regards the Law of Return. They will demand a law of return for the Palestinians. The Law of Return for the Jews does not bring great numbers of Jews here, but the law of return for the Palestinians may bring large numbers. And, therefore, Israel would stop being a country in which Jews constitute the majority. A binational state would be a very uneasy state. I don't consider the Jews and the Arabs capable of living together in peace like Switzerland; perhaps in the distant future.

Harkabi then goes on to argue, "I adhere to the Zionist idea that the Jews should have a country of their very own. But it can't be a big country. It can be only a small country. Therefore my version of Zionism is Zionism of quality, not a Zionism of acreage."[2] Of course, opponents of this view would take the position that given the size of Israel to begin with, it is rather absurd to argue about Israel becoming a "big country" if it retains the West Bank.

A second objection is that to preserve Jewish dominance of the state, it would become necessary to suppress the national desire of the Palestinian Arabs to attain political sovereignty over their own land. Thus, were Israel to decide to annex Judea and Samaria, it would have to be prepared to adopt a form of political apartheid which would place the Arabs of Israel in a permanent status of second-class citizens, with severe limitations on their political freedoms. Presumably, the Arabs of Israel would then seek ways of protesting such political suppression that would of necessity lead to a cycle of ever more militant suppression and protest. Such a situation would both corrupt the moral nature of Israel as a Jewish state and seriously undermine the nation's morale. It is presumed that most Israeli Jews would be unwilling to accept the idea of Jewish suppression of their Arab neighbors.

The alternative of establishing an independent Arab state in the West Bank is opposed by both Israel and Jordan, but for radically different reasons. The predominant view in Israel is that such an Arab state would be intrinsically unviable and would serve to destabilize the region. Furthermore, since the Arab population of the West Bank, notwithstanding the present Israeli control, which has allowed substantially greater freedoms there than were ever realized under Jordanian rule, has proven itself incapable of developing an independent indigenous leadership, such a state would come under the radical control of the PLO, which would use it as a base for harassing and ultimately undermining the quality of life in Israel. Since the PLO has clearly indicated repeatedly that its goal is the "liberation of all of Palestine," there is no basis whatever for arguing that if it were given the West Bank it would develop a different and more responsible set of political aims and priorities. Compounding the problem is the fact that, given the size of the present West Bank population, the establishment of a Palestinian state there would leave unresolved the question of the Palestinian diaspora. It is unlikely that even a fraction of the Palestinians spread throughout the Arab world would be able to be reabsorbed in the limited territory available without creating new conditions of instability and a demand for lebensraum. Finally, there is a fear that such a PLO state would ally itself with the Soviet Union and other radical states that might serve as a counterweight to Israel's military superiority, thus further complicating Israel's ability to protect its national interests.

There is also a school of thought in Israel that is vehemently opposed to the idea of granting independence to the West Bank

Afterword

because this would simply be creating a *second* Arab state in Palestine. One of the more forceful exponents of this view is Ariel Sharon. During his discussions with President Carter in March 1979 regarding an Egyptian-Israeli peace settlement, Sharon is reported to have made his position on the West Bank clear to the president:

> There *is* now a Palestinian state. It is called Jordan. It consists of three-fourths of the land mass of Palestine as determined by the League of Nations. . . . Of the 2 million people living in Jordan, nearly all are Palestinians. If you count the Bedouins as Palestinians—and why not, they were born there—then everyone in Jordan is a Palestinian, except maybe the Hashemite King Hussein, because his dynasty was imported by the British from Arabia. So a Palestinian state on the West Bank would be a *second* Palestinian state.[3]

As demonstrated earlier, Jordan has always been adamantly opposed to an independent Arab state in the West Bank as a threat to Hashemite rule. Since the majority of Jordanians are of Palestinian extraction, there is a well-founded fear that such a Palestinian entity would be a serious and probably victorious competitor for the allegiance of the majority of Jordanians. This might ultimately result in the overthrow of the Hashemites and the transformation of the West and East banks into a Palestinian republic.

The "Jordan Option" has gained acceptability among a good part of the Israeli public and is actively promoted by the country's Labor party constituency. It is argued that only such an accommodation can satisfactorily resolve the problems posed to the political and moral integrity of Israel as a democratic state and society by its rule over the heavily Arab-populated West Bank. In principle, this is what Jordan has been seeking ever since it lost control over the West Bank. The fundamental issue between Jordan and those in Israel favoring the Jordan Option concerns the terms under which the territories would be returned to Jordanian sovereignty. Jordan's basic position is that all of the West Bank, including East Jerusalem, must be returned in exchange for peace. This position was reaffirmed in the spring of

Afterword

1987 by Mohamed Kamal, Jordan's amabassador to Washington, in the following terms:

> In practical terms, the prospects for peace depend on the mutual Arab and Israeli recognition of three basic principles: That the occupation of land and hegemony over people by force is inadmissible. That peace can only be negotiated with the participation of all parties involved in the conflict, including the Palestinians. That every country in the region, including Israel, must be guaranteed the security of its sovereign existence. . . . As long as Israel refuses to relinquish the West Bank and Gaza—lands it has held under military occupation since 1967—as long as it refuses to recognize the legitimate rights of the 1.3 million Palestinians who live under its oppression and the millions of others living in diaspora around the world—it will find no peace or security. Preoccupation with security based on military might and the acquisition of land will never assure Israel's future. Only the restoration of Palestinian rights in a land of their own will bring the just and lasting peace needed to release Israel from its fortress of fear and guarantee its permanent security.[4]

Of course, this notion of "Palestinian rights in a land of their own" must be understood to mean local autonomy within the context of Hussein's federation plan and not sovereign independence.

The position of those Israelis who are proponents of an accommodation with Jordan has been that only the Arab-populated sectors would be returned, with special security arrangements made for continued Israeli control of the frontier as it now stands. This clearly means something less than absolute Jordanian sovereignty over the area. Furthermore, the return of East Jerusalem, notwithstanding its great symbolic importance to the Hashemites, is out of the question as far as even the most accommodation-minded mainstream Israelis are concerned. However, even with regard to Jerusalem, there are some who would be prepared to grant Jordan theoretical sovereignty over the Muslim holy places, to be symbolized by permitting the Jordanian flag to be flown at the sites.

Although the viability of the Jordan Option has been called into serious question as a result of Hussein's July 31, 1988 disavowal of further claims on the West Bank, it continues to be considered as a realistic alternative by many who argue that

Hussein's statement should not be taken overly seriously; that is, that he is in no position simply to write off the Palestinians without putting his regime at critical risk.

Opposition to the Jordan Option in Israel comes not only from the mainstream nationalist-religious circles. It also comes from the small constituency that favors a separate Palestinian state in the West Bank for its indigenous population. This view argues that the Palestinian Arabs have never accepted Jordanian rule, and that it is unreasonable for Israel to compel them to do so. Furthermore, the advocates of this view see Jordan as an unreliable and untrustworthy neighbor that should not be rewarded for its bungled attempts to create an expanded Hashemite state at Israel's, as well as the Palestinians', expense. This position was perhaps best articulated by Mattityahu Peled, who argued as early as 1969 against Israel's Labor government's readiness to resolve the problems resulting from the occupation of the West Bank by returning most of the territories to Jordanian rule. "We must ask," he wrote, "should the West Bank be returned to Hussein in exchange for a peace treaty?" He questioned, as many Israelis of a variety of political persuasions have also done, whether the Hashemites have ever really sought peace. "The legend that Abdullah paid with his life for attempting to make peace with Israel is not true. He never tried and never intended to make peace with Israel. Rather, Abdullah was murdered because he invaded the West Bank and annexed it to his Emirate, thereby putting an end to the aspirations and hopes of the West Bank Palestinian Arabs to attain their own political independence."

Peled further pointed out that Abdullah and Hussein had to go to great expense to build dozens of military encampments on the West Bank that effectively surrounded all the main population centers, not for the purpose of establishing a strong defense line against Israel but rather "in order to insure their rule over the hostile population. . . . The Jordanian rulers have always been aware that the integrity of their kingdom depended more on the subjugation of the West Bank population than on the strength of their fortified posts on Israel's border. For that reason they concentrated a large force to encircle West Bank towns and the important village concentrations with security belts, and cruelly

Afterword

crushed any attempt at protest by the conquered population." Indeed, he argued, notwithstanding the distastefulness of an Israeli military occupation government ruling over a hostile Arab population, "the internal security problems of the Israeli military on the West Bank are incomparably easier to cope with than those which confronted the earlier Jordanian military rule."[5]

Many observers would maintain that this assessment remains essentially valid notwithstanding the outbreak of the *intafada*, a relatively low level although widely publicized campaign of resistance against Israeli control of the West Bank and Gaza, in late 1987.

As with the other options, that of maintaining the status quo also has its advocates and opponents. For some supporters of the Likud position regarding Judea and Samaria, given the political impracticability of annexing the territories for the reasons discussed earlier, perpetuation of the status quo becomes the least objectionable alternative. Those who prefer this arrangement for the foreseeable future are fully sensitive to the negative effect that the occupation has had on Israeli morale, but nonetheless insist that it is a price that must be paid in the national interest. Some would even argue that, as a practical matter, the West Bankers are probably better off the way they are than they would be under a renewed occupation by Jordan. The problem with this argument is, of course, that since the West Bank has been under Israeli control for more than twenty years, the younger generation has no recollection of Jordan's repressive rule for the two decades before 1967.

Advocates of this position might also argue that, notwithstanding Jordan's insistence on the return of the entire West Bank as the price for peace, Israel has already enjoyed a de facto peace with Jordan since 1970. In this view, a formal de jure peace treaty with Jordan would not add anything worth paying very much for. Perpetuation of the status quo in the West Bank therefore does not affect the realities of war and peace among the states of the Middle East. Indeed, many Israelis today feel that the price paid in territory for the peace treaty with Egypt was both unnecessary and excessive. In their view, it is not the treaty that has prevented Egypt from renewing hostilities with Israel; it is rather that it is not in Egypt's interests to do so at this point. They are

Afterword

convinced that should Egypt's self-definition of its interests change, the Camp David accord will not have much deterrent effect. A treaty does not create peace, it only memorializes it. In the case of Jordan, the piece of paper would have even less tangible redemption value, since the country is not now, nor is it ever likely to be, in a position to undertake a unilateral decision for war. Thus, while it would be nice to have formal peace treaties with all of its neighbors, Israel must evaluate their significance in real rather than symbolic terms. From this standpoint, Hussein has really nothing to offer in exchange for the territories he demands.

Opposition in Israel to the perpetuation of the status quo is led primarily by the Labor and liberal fringe parties that see continued occupation of the West Bank as destructive to Israel's national morality and as a stain on its history. This position is reflected in the zeal with which the political leaders of these parties and factions advocate the "Jordan Option" as the only viable solution to Israel's dilemma.

From Hussein's perspective, the perpetuation of the status quo could mean a hastening of the end of Hashemite rule in Jordan. As the ability of the PLO to realize its goal of the liberation of Palestine continues to diminish, there is the distinct possibility that it might resolve ultimately to shift its focus to the "Jordan is Palestine" solution and provoke an anti-Hashemite revolution among the Palestinian majority in the country. Of course, the PLO would retain its rhetoric concerning the return of the Palestinians to their homes in what is now Israel as it proceeded to accept Palestine east of the Jordan as the Palestinian homeland. It would remain irredentist with regard to Israel, but might well reach an acceptable practical accommodation as it faced the everyday realities of running a modern national state. Hussein thus continues to proclaim at every opportunity that time is running out for peace in the Middle East. However, it would appear that, with or without the resolution of the West Bank problem on Hussein's terms, time may be running out not for peace but for the Hashemites.

The issues preventing a satisfactory resolution of the gnawing problem of the West Bank are fundamental and preclude easy reconciliation or accommodation. Given the prevailing realities, it

Afterword

appears most likely, at least to this observer, that the status quo will be perpetuated for the foreseeable future, notwithstanding the impact this may have for the future of Hashemite Jordan. From a historical perspective, preservation of the status quo in the West Bank may be seen as perhaps the penultimate phase of the long-standing Hashemite-Zionist struggle for Palestine.

Notes

Chapter 1. The Anglo-Hashemite Conspiracy
1. Quoted in James Morris, *The Hashemite Kings*, p. 10.
2. Quoted in Elie Kedourie, *In the Anglo-Arab Labyrinth*, p. 5.
3. Morris, op. cit., p. 15.
4. Quoted from German documents in Jon Kimche, *The Second Arab Awakening*, p. 32.
5. Quoted in Kedourie, op. cit., p. 5.
6. Ibid., p. 7.
7. Ibid., p. 15.
8. Ibid., p.. 17.
9. A. L. Tibawi, *Anglo-Arab Relations and the Question of Palestine 1914–1921*, p. 51.
10. Quoted in Kedourie, op. cit., p. 18.
11. Ibid., p. 19.
12. Quoted in Briton Cooper Busch, *Britain, India, and the Arabs, 1914–1921*, p. 62.
13. Kimche, op. cit., p. 34.
14. George Antonius, *The Arab Awakening*, pp. 140–42.
15. Ibid., pp. 157–58.
16. Quoted in Isaiah Friedman, *The Question of Palestine, 1915–1918*, p. 67.
17. Ronald Storrs, *Orientations*, p. 161.
18. Antonius, op. cit., p. 416. The complete Hussein-McMahon correspondence is included in the appendixes to Antonius's book.
19. Quoted in Busch, op. cit., p. 92.

Notes

20. Quoted in Kedourie, "Cairo and Khartoum on the Arab Question," *Historical Journal* VII (1964) 2.
21. Quoted in Friedman, op. cit., p. 73.
22. Ibid., pp. 73–74. Friedman takes issue with Antonius's translation, which he considers as "faulty and distorts the meaning of McMahon's intention" (p. 352, n. 38).
23. Quoted ibid., p. 68.
24. Ibid., pp. 95–96.
25. Antonius, op. cit., p. 188.
26. Quoted in Howard M. Sachar, *The Emergence of the Middle East: 1914–1924*, p. 130.
27. Quoted in Antonius, op. cit., p. 190.
28. Quoted in Sachar, op. cit., p. 130.
29. Quoted in Friedman, op. cit., p. 78.
30. Quoted in Kedourie, *In the Anglo-Arab Labyrinth*, p. 147.
31. T. E. Lawrence, *Secret Dispatches from Arabia*, p. 39.
32. Lawrence, *Seven Pillars of Wisdom*, p. 571.
33. Quoted in Kedourie, *England and the Middle East*, p. 39.
34. B. H. Liddell Hart, *"T. E. Lawrence"—In Arabia and After*, p. 201.
35. Richard Aldington, *Lawrence of Arabia*, p. 210.
36. David Lloyd George, *The Truth about the Peace Treaties*, p. 1047.
37. Quoted in Antonius, op. cit., pp. 433–34.
38. Quoted in Kedourie, op. cit., p. 21.
39. Kedourie, *The Chatham House Version and Other Middle Eastern Studies*, p. 51.

Chapter 2. The Anglo-Zionist Conspiracy

1. Marvin Lowenthal, ed., *The Diaries of Theodor Herzl*, p. 152.
2. Israel Zangwill, "Nordau," *The Jewish Standard*, January 28, 1944.
3. Quoted in Nevill Barbour, *Nisi Dominus*, p. 52.
4. Quoted in Adolph Böhm, *Die Zionistische Bewegung*, vol. 1, p. 293.
5. Quoted in Nahum M. Gelber, *Hatzharat Balfour veToldoteha*, p. 190.
6. Isaiah Friedman, *Germany, Turkey and Zionism 1897–1918*, p. 213.
7. Howard M. Sachar, *The Emergence of the Middle East: 1914–1924*, pp. 192–93.
8. Gelber, op. cit., p. 162.
9. Sachar, *A History of Israel*, p. 91.
10. H. F. Frischwasser-Ra'anan, *The Frontiers of a Nation*, pp. 28–30.
11. Quoted in Friedman, *The Question of Palestine, 1914–1918*, p. 111.
12. Quoted in Jon Kimche, *The Unromantics*, pp. 26–28.
13. Friedman, op. cit., pp. 53–59.

14. Ibid., p. 54.
15. Ibid., p. 53.
16. Quoted in Kimche, *The Second Arab Awakening*, p. 54.
17. Ibid., p. 55.
18. Leonard Stein, *The Balfour Declaration*, p. 392.
19. Quoted in Frischwasser-Ra'anan, op. cit., p. 77.
20. Ibid., p. 78.
21. Quoted in Friedman, op. cit., p. 114.
22. Quoted in Kimche, op. cit., p. 60.
23. Quoted in Frischwasser-Ra'anan, op. cit., p. 83.
24. Quoted in Stein, op. cit., p. 462.
25. Ibid., p. 470.
26. Quoted in Kimche, op. cit., p. 63.
27. Ibid.
28. Quoted in Stein, op. cit., p. 528.
29. David Lloyd George, *The Truth About the Peace Treaties*, p. 1126.
30. Quoted in Kimche, op. cit., p. 64.
31. David Lloyd George, *Memoirs of the Peace Conference*, vol. II, p. 737.
32. Palestine Royal Commission, *Report*, p. 23.
33. Quoted in Isaiah Friedman, *Germany, Turkey and Zionism*, pp. 382–83.
34. John H. Patterson, Foreword to Vladimir Jabotinsky, *The Story of the Jewish Legion*, p. 21.
35. Quoted in Kimche, *The Unromantics*, p. 52.
36. Ibid., pp. 53–54.
37. Ibid., pp. 55–56.

Chapter 3. The Period of Hashemite-Zionist Cooperation

1. David Lloyd George, *Memoirs of the Peace Conference*, vol. II, p. 1038.
2. H. H. Cumming, *Franco-British Rivalry in the Post-War Near East*, p. 58.
3. Chaim Weizmann, *The Letters and Papers of Chaim Weizmann*, vol. VIII, p. 210.
4. Weizmann, *Trial and Error*, p. 234.
5. Quoted in Jon Kimche, *There Could Have Been Peace*, p. 58.
6. Quoted in John J. McTague, *British Policy in Palestine, 1917–1922*, p. 53.
7. Quoted in Kimche, *The Unromantics*, p. 64.
8. Ibid., p. 67.
9. *Jewish Chronicle* (London), November 1, 1918.
10. Weizmann, *Letters and Papers*, vol. IX, p. 15, n. 8.
11. Ibid., pp. 12–13.
12. Ibid., pp. 70–71.
13. Ibid., pp. 71–72.

Notes

14. Frank E. Manuel, *The Realities of American-Palestine Relations*, p. 204.
15. Ibid., p. 134.
16. Quoted in Elie Kedourie, *In the Anglo-Arab Labyrinth*, p. 222.
17. Full facsimile text of agreement in Weizmann, *Letters and Papers*, vol. IX, between pp. 86 and 87.
18. A. L. Tibawi, *Anglo-Arab Relations and the Question of Palestine 1914–1921*, pp. 332–36, 342–43.
19. George Antonius, *The Arab Awakening*, p. 285.
20. H. F. Frischwasser-Ra'anan, *The Frontiers of a Nation*, p. 105.
21. Ibid., p. 107.
22. Quoted in Kedourie, op. cit., p. 222.
23. Paul L. Hanna, *British Policy in Palestine*, p. 50.
24. Quoted in Aharon Cohen, *Israel and the Arab World*, p. 143.
25. Quoted in Hanna, op. cit., pp. 51–52.
26. Weizmann, op. cit., p. 119, n. 7.
27. Quoted in Richard Meinertzhagen, *Middle East Diary 1917–1956*, pp. 15–16.
28. Quoted in Bernard Joseph, *British Rule in Palestine*, p. 25.
29. *Documents on British Foreign Policy*, 1st Series, vol. IV, p. 265.
30. Quoted in Abu Khaldun Sati al-Husri, *The Day of Maysalun*, p. 131.
31. *Documents on British Foreign Policy*, op. cit., pp. 364–65.
32. Ibid., p. 368.
33. Ibid., pp. 421–22.
34. Weizmann, op. cit., pp. 230–31.
35. *Documents on British Foreign Policy*, op cit., p. 608.
36. Quoted in al-Husri, op. cit., p. 49.
37. Weizmann, op. cit., p. 328.
38. Howard M. Sachar, *The Emergence of the Middle East: 1914–1924*, p. 275.
39. Quoted in Kimche, *There Could Have Been Peace*, p. 208.
40. Quoted in Friedman, op. cit., p. 95.

Chapter 4. The Emergence of Hashemite Transjordan

1. H. F. Frischwasser-Ra'anan, *The Frontiers of a Nation*, p. 121.
2. Benjamin Shwadran, *Jordan a State of Tension*, p. 123.
3. Quoted in Uriel Dann, *Studies in the History of Transjordan, 1920–1949*, pp. 18–19.
4. Alec Kirkbride, *A Crackle of Thorns*, p. 19.
5. Quoted in Aaron S. Klieman, *Foundations of British Policy in the Arab World*, p. 74.
6. Ibid., p. 75.
7. Jon Kimche, *The Second Arab Awakening*, p. 155.
8. Quoted in Dann, op. cit., pp. 25–26.

9. Chaim Weizmann, *The Letters and Papers of Chaim Weizmann*, Vol. X, pp. 159–62.
10. Shwadran, op. cit., p. 132.
11. Dann, op. cit., pp. 37–40.
12. *Documents on British Foreign Policy*, First Series, vol. IV, p. 302.
13. Ibid., p. 347.
14. Abdullah, King of Jordan, *My Memoirs Completed*, pp. 91–92.
15. Richard Meinertzhagen, *Middle East Diary 1917–1956*, p. 100.
16. Quoted in Nevill Barbour, *Nisi Dominus*, p. 104, n. 1.
17. Kirkbride, op. cit., p. 27.
18. Quoted in Lewis B. Namier, *In the Margin of History*, p. 282.
19. Aharon Cohen, *Israel and the Arab World*, pp. 190–91.
20. Quoted in Neil Caplan, *Futile Diplomacy*, p. 53.
21. Quoted in Shwadran, op. cit., pp. 141–42.
22. Royal Institute of International Affairs, *Great Britain and Palestine 1915–1945*, p. 16.
23. Quoted in Cohen, op. cit., p. 190.
24. Ibid., p. 192.
25. *New York Times*, July 18, 1933.
26. From minutes of the meeting, quoted in Cohen, op. cit., pp. 253–54.
27. Shwadran, op. cit., pp. 190–92.
28. Quoted in Cohen, op. cit., p. 191.
29. Palestine Royal Commission, *Report*, p. 381.
30. Quoted in *Survey of International Affairs 1937*, vol. I, p. 551.
31. *Palestine: A Study of Jewish, Arab and British Policies*, vol. II, p. 857.
32. Quoted in George E. Kirk, *A Short History of the Middle East*, pp. 160–61.
33. Ibid., p. 160.
34. Golda Meir, *My Life*, p. 215.
35. John B. Glubb, *A Soldier with the Arabs*, p. 63.
36. Ibid., p. 152.
37. Larry Collins and Dominique Lapierre, *O Jerusalem!*, pp. 329–32.
38. Meir, op. cit., pp. 218–19.
39. David Ben-Gurion, *Israel: A Personal History*, p. 91.
40. Kirkbride, *From the Wings*, pp. 21–22.
41. Quoted in Clinton Bailey, "Changing Attitudes Toward Jordan in the West Bank," *Middle East Journal*, Spring 1978, p. 155.
42. Glubb, op. cit., p. 96.
43. Ibid., p. 79.
44. Abdullah, op. cit. p. 30.

Notes

Chapter 5. From Transjordan to Jordan and Back

1. Benjamin Shwadran, *Jordan a State of Tension*, p. 280.
2. Quoted in Hussein A. Hassouna, *The League of Arab States and Regional Disputes*, p. 33.
3. Shwadran, op. cit., p. 282.
4. Ibid., pp. 282–83.
5. Ibid., p. 286, n. 9.
6. Walter Eytan, *The First Ten Years*, pp. 42–43.
7. Moshe Dayan, *Moshe Dayan*, pp. 143–44.
8. Ibid., p. 133.
9. Aharon Cohen, *Israel and the Arab World*, p. 474.
10. Quoted in Shwadran, op. cit., p. 292.
11. Ibid., p. 296.
12. Abdullah, *My Memoirs Completed*, p. 22.
13. Quoted in Marjorie M. Whiteman, *Digest of International Law*, vol. 2., p. 1166.
14. Hassouna, op. cit., p. 40.
15. Quoted in Walter Laqueur, *The Road to Jerusalem*, p. 53.
16. Yehoshafat Harkabi, *The Palestinian Covenant and Its Meaning*, p. 111.
17. Donald Neff, *Warriors for Jerusalem*, pp. 33–34.
18. Zeev Schiff and Raphael Rothstein, *Fedayeen*, p. 63.
19. Ibid.
20. Vick Vance and Pierre Lauer, *Hussein King of Jordan*, pp. 21–22.
21. Quoted in David Kimche and Dan Bawly, *The Sandstorm*, p. 103.
22. Vance and Lauer, op. cit., p. 33.
23. Quoted in Laqueur, op. cit., p. 92.
24. Vance and Lauer, op. cit., p. 34.
25. Peter Snow, *Hussein*, p. 173.
26. Ibid., p. 176.
27. Israel Ministry of Defense, *The Six Days' War*, p. 85.
28. Quoted in Theodore Draper, *Israel and World Politics*, p. 115; see also Odd Bull, *War and Peace in the Middle East*, p. 113.
29. Draper, op. cit., p. 115.
30. Vance and Lauer, op. cit., p. 65.
31. Ibid., p. 80.
32. Ibid., p. 65n.
33. Ibid., p. 126.

Chapter 6. Hussein, the Palestinians and Israel

1. Gideon Rafael, *Destination Peace*, p. 197.

Notes

2. Yehuda Lukacs, ed., *Documents on the Israeli-Palestinian Conflict 1967–1983*, p. 147.
3. Ahmad Baha al-Din, *Iqtirah dawlat Filistin* (Beirut, 1968), reprinted in Anouar Abdel-Malek, ed., *Contemporary Arab Political Thought*, p. 199.
4. Aziz Shihadeh, "Must History Repeat Itself?" In Shlomo Avineri, ed., *Israel and the Palestinians*, p. 54.
5. Mattityahu Peled, "Palestinian or Jordanian Entity?" In Avineri, op. cit., pp. 34–35.
6. Zeev Schiff and Raphael Rothstein, *Fedayeen*, p. 75.
7. Ibid., p. 107.
8. *New York Times*, November 3, 1968.
9. *International Documents on Palestine 1970*, p. 795.
10. "The Palestinians and Israel," in Avineri, op. cit., pp. 151–52.
11. Yitzhak Rabin, *The Rabin Memoirs*, p. 187.
12. Rafael, op. cit., pp. 246–47.
13. Rabin, op. cit., p. 189.
14. *International Documents on Palestine 1971*, p. 398.
15. Quoted by Anne Sinai and Allen Pollack, eds., *The Hashemite Kingdom of Jordan and the West Bank*, pp. 131–35.
16. Quoted in Shaul Mishal, *The PLO Under Arafat*, p. 140.
17. Lukacs, op. cit., p. 154.
18. Ibid., p. 222.
19. Rafael, op. cit., p. 321.
20. Moshe Dayan, *Moshe Dayan*, pp. 432–33.
21. Mishal, ibid.
22. *Washington Post*, November 12, 1979.
23. See Lukacs, op. cit., p. 223.
24. Quoted by Arye Naor, "From Occupation to Confederation," *Viewpoints*, March 22, 1987, p. 3.
25. Jimmy Carter, *Keeping Faith*, p. 300.
26. *Jordan Times*, May 9, 1981.
27. *Le Monde*, March 8, 1980.
28. Mishal, op. cit., p. 146; see also Helena Cobban, *The Palestinian Liberation Organization*, p. 118.
29. *New York Times*, November 27, 1982.
30. Interview on BBC-TV on September 13, quoted in *The New York Times*, September 15, 1982.
31. Quoted in Mishal, op. cit., p. 169.

Afterword

1. Arye Naor, "From Occupation to Confederation," *Viewpoints*, March 22, 1987, p. 4.

Notes

2. Interview with Salim Tamari, *Journal of Palestine Studies*, Spring 1987, pp. 46–47.

3. *New York Times Magazine*, April 8, 1979.

4. Mohamed Kamal, "An Arab's Peace Plea: We Need Jewish Help," *Washington Post*, April 19, 1987.

5. Mattityahu Peled, "Palestinian or Jordanian Entity?" In Shlomo Avineri, ed., *Israel and the Palestinians*, pp. 32–34.

Bibliography

Abdel-Malek, Anouar, ed. *Contemporary Arab Political Thought.* London, 1983.
Abdullah, King of Jordan, *Memoirs.* London, 1950.
———. *My Memoirs Completed.* Washington, 1954.
Ajami, Fouad. *The Arab Predicament.* New York, 1981.
———. "The Revolution That Failed." *The Nation,* May 9, 1981.
Aldington, Richard. *Lawrence of Arabia, A Biographical Enquiry.* 2nd ed. London, 1969.
Alexander, Yonah, and Nicholas N. Kittrie, eds. *Crescent and Star.* New York, 1973.
Alroy, Gil Carl. *Behind the Middle East Conflict.* New York, 1975.
Antonius, George. *The Arab Awakening.* New York, 1965.
Atiyah, Edward. *The Arabs.* Baltimore, 1958.
Avineri, Shlomo, ed. *Israel and the Palestinians.* New York, 1971.
Bailey, Clinton. "Changing Attitudes Toward Jordan in the West Bank." *Middle East Journal,* Spring 1978.
Barbour, Nevill. *Nisi Dominus: A Survey of the Palestine Controversy.* Beirut, 1969.
Becker, Jillian. *The PLO.* London, 1984.
Ben-Gurion, David. *Israel: A Personal History.* New York, 1971.
Böhm, Adolph. *Die Zionistische Bewegung.* Vol. 1, Tel Aviv, 1935, Vol. 2, Jerusalem, 1937.
Bull, Odd. *War and Peace in the Middle East.* London, 1976.

Bibliography

Busch, Briton Cooper. *Britain, India, and the Arabs, 1914–1918.* Berkeley, 1971.
Campbell, John C. "The Arab-Israeli Conflict: An American Policy." *Foreign Affairs,* October 1970.
Caplan, Neil. *Futile Diplomacy: Early Arab-Zionist Negotiation Attempts 1913–1931.* London, 1983.
Carter, Jimmy. *Keeping Faith: The Memoirs of a President.* New York, 1982.
Childers, Ernest B. "Impasse in the Holy Land." *Encounter,* July 1958.
Cobban, Helena. *The Palestinian Liberation Organization.* Cambridge, 1984.
Cohen, Aharon. *Israel and the Arab World.* New York, 1970.
Collins, Larry, and Dominique Lapierre. *O Jerusalem!* New York, 1972.
Cumming, H. H. *Franco-British Rivalry in the Post-War Near East.* Oxford, 1938.
Dann, Uriel. *Studies in the History of Transjordan, 1920–1949: The Making of a State.* Boulder, 1984.
Dayan, Moshe. *Moshe Dayan: Story of My Life.* New York, 1976.
Documents on British Foreign Policies. 1st Series. Vol. IV.
Draper, Theodore. *Israel and World Politics.* New York, 1944.
Eytan, Walter. *The First Ten Years: A Diplomatic History of Israel.* New York, 1958.
Frankenstein, Ernst. *Justice for My People.* New York, 1944.
Friedman, Isaiah. *Germany, Turkey and Zionism 1897–1918.* Oxford, 1977.
——— . *The Question of Palestine, 1914–1918: British-Jewish-Arab Relations.* New York, 1973.
Frischwasser-Ra'anan, H. F. *The Frontiers of a Nation.* London, 1955.
Gabrieli, Francesco. *The Arab Revival.* New York, 1961.
Gelber, Nahum M. *Hatzharat Balfour veToldoteha.* Jerusalem, 1939.
Gilbert, Martin. *Britain, Palestine and the Jews.* Oxford Centre for Postgraduate Hebrew Studies, 1977.
Glubb, John B. *A Soldier with the Arabs.* New York, 1957.
Gruen, George, C., ed. *The Palestinians in Perspective.* New York, 1982.
Hanna, Paul L. *British Policy in Palestine.* Washington, 1942.
Harkabi, Yehoshafat. *The Palestinian Covenant and Its Meaning.* London, 1979.
Hassan bin Talal. *Search for Peace.* London, 1984.
Hassouna, Hussein A. *The League of Arab States and Regional Disputes.* Leiden, 1975.
Hourani, Cecil. "The Moment of Truth." *Encounter,* November 1967.
Howe, Irving, and Carl Gershman, eds. *Israel, the Arabs and the Middle East.* New York, 1972.
Hudson, Michael C. *Arab Politics: The Search for Legitimacy.* New Haven, 1980.
al-Husri, Abu Khaldun Sati. *The Day of Maysalun.* Washington, 1966.
Hussein, King of Jordan. *Uneasy Lies the Head.* New York, 1962.

Bibliography

Ingrams, Doreen. *Palestine Papers 1917–1922: Seeds of Conflict.* New York, 1973.
International Documents on Palestine 1970. Beirut, 1973.
International Documents on Palestine 1971. Beirut, 1974.
Israel Ministry of Defense. *The Six Days' War. 1967.*
Jabotinsky, Vladimir. *The Story of the Jewish Legion.* New York, 1945.
Jasse, Richard L. "Great Britain and Abdallah's Plan to Partition Palestine: A 'Natural Sorting Out,'" *Middle Eastern Studies,* October 1986.
Joseph, Bernard. *British Rule in Palestine.* Washington, 1948.
Kamal, Mohamed. "An Arab's Peace Plea: We Need Jewish Help." *Washington Post,* April 19, 1987.
Kazziha, Walid W. *Palestine in the Arab Dilemma.* London, 1979.
Kedourie, Elie. "Cairo and Khartoum on the Arab Question." *Historical Journal VII,* no. 2 (1964).
———. *The Chatham House Version and Other Middle Eastern Studies.* London, 1970.
———. *England and the Middle East.* Hassocks, Sussex, 1978.
———. *In the Anglo-Arab Labyrinth.* Cambridge, 1976.
Kerr, Malcolm H. *The Arab Cold War.* New York, 1975.
Kimche, David and Dan Bawly. *The Sandstorm: The Arab-Israeli War of 1967: Prelude and Aftermath.* New York, 1968.
Kimche, Jon. *The Second Arab Awakening.* New York, 1970.
———. *There Could Have Been Peace.* New York, 1973.
———. *The Unromantics: The Great Powers and the Balfour Declaration.* London, 1968.
Kirk, George E. *A Short History of the Middle East.* Washington, 1949.
Kirkbride, Alec. *A Crackle of Thorns.* London, 1956.
———. *From the Wings: Amman Memoirs, 1947–1951.* London, 1976.
Klieman, Aaron S. *Foundations of British Policy in the Arab World: The Cairo Conference of 1921.* Baltimore, 1970.
Knox, D. Edward. *The Making of a New Eastern Question: British Palestine Policy and the Origins of Israel, 1917–1925.* Washington, 1981.
Laqueur, Walter. *The Road to Jerusalem.* New York, 1968.
Lawrence, T. E. *Secret Dispatches from Arabia.* London, 1939.
Liddell Hart, B. H. *"T. E. Lawrence"—In Arabia and After.* London, 1936.
———. *Seven Pillars of Wisdom.* Garden City, N.Y., 1935.
Lloyd George, David. *Memoirs of the Peace Conference.* Vol. II. London, 1938.
———. *The Truth about the Peace Treaties.* London, 1936.
Lowenthal, Marvin, ed. *The Diaries of Theodor Herzl.* New York, 1956.
Lukacs, Yehuda, ed. *Documents on the Israeli-Palestinian Conflict 1967–1983.* Cambridge, 1984.

McTague, John J. *British Policy in Palestine, 1917–1922.* Lanham, Maryland, 1983.
Mansfield, Peter. *The Arabs.* New York, 1983.
Manuel, Frank E. *The Realities of American-Palestine Relations.* Washington, 1949.
Marlowe, John. *The Seat of Pilate.* London, 1959.
Meinertzhagen, Richard. *Middle East Diary 1917–1956.* New York, 1960.
Meir, Golda. *My Life.* New York, 1975.
Miller, Aaron D. *The Arab States and the Palestine Question.* New York, 1986.
Mishal, Shaul. *The PLO under 'Arafat: Between Gun and Olive Branch.* New Haven, 1986.
Morris, James. *The Hashemite Kings.* New York, 1959.
Namier, Lewis B. *In the Margin of History.* Freeport, N.Y. 1969.
Naor, Arye. "From Occupation to Confederation: A Framework for Comprehensive Peace Between Israel and Its Neighbors." *Viewpoints* (Jerusalem, Center for Public Affairs), March 22, 1987.
Neff, Donald. *Warriors for Jerusalem: The Six Days That Changed the Middle East.* New York, 1984.
Palestine: A Study of Jewish, Arab and British Policies. 2 vols. New Haven, 1947.
Palestine Royal Commission. *Report.* London, 1937.
Pearlman, Moshe. "Chapters of Arab-Jewish Diplomacy, 1918–1922." *Jewish Social Studies* VI, April 1944.
Polk, William R. *The Arab World.* Cambridge, Mass., 1981.
Porath, Yehoshua. "Abdallah's Greater Syria Programme." *Middle Eastern Studies,* April 1984.
Prittie, Terence. *Eshkol: The Man and the Nation.* New York, 1969.
Rabin, Yitzhak. *The Rabin Memoirs.* Boston, 1979.
Rafael, Gideon. *Destination Peace: Three Decades of Israeli Foreign Policy.* New York, 1981.
Riad, Mahmoud. *The Struggle for Peace in the Middle East.* London, 1981.
Royal Institute of International Affairs. *Great Britain and Palestine 1915–1945.* London, 1946.
Sachar, Howard M. *The Emergence of the Middle East: 1914–1924.* New York, 1969.
———. *A History of Israel.* New York, 1976.
Samuel, Herbert L. *Grooves of Change: A Book of Memoirs.* Indianapolis, 1946.
Sanders, Ronald. *The High Walls of Jerusalem.* New York, 1984.
Satloff, Robert B. *Troubles on the East Bank.* New York, 1986.
Schiff, Zeev, and Raphael Rothstein. *Fedayeen: Guerrillas Against Israel.* New York, 1972.
Sereni, Enzo, and R. E. Ashery, eds. *Jews and Arabs in Palestine.* New York, 1936.

Bibliography

Shemesh, Moshe. "The Founding of the PLO 1984." *Middle Eastern Studies*, October 1984.

Shwadran, Benjamin. *Jordan a State of Tension*. New York, 1959.

Sinai, Anne, and Allen Pollack, eds. *The Hashemite Kingdom of Jordan and the West Bank*. New York, 1977.

Snow, Peter. *Hussein*. London, 1972.

Storrs, Ronald. *Orientations*. London, 1937.

Stein, Leonard. *The Balfour Declaration*. New York, 1961.

Stoyanovsky, J. *The Mandate for Palestine*. London, 1928.

Survey of International Affairs 1937. 2 vols. London, 1938.

Sykes, Christopher. *Crossroads to Israel*. Cleveland, 1965.

Tamari, Salim. Interview: "Yehoshafat Harkabi: Choosing Between Bad and Worse." *Journal of Palestine Studies*, Spring 1987.

Taylor, Alan R. *The Arab Balance of Power*. Syracuse, 1982.

Tibawi, A. L. *Anglo-Arab Relations and the Question of Palestine 1914–1921*. London, 1978.

Tuma, Elias H. "The Arabs in Israel: An Impasse." *New Outlook*, March–April 1966.

———. *Peacemaking and the Immoral War: Arabs and Jews in the Middle East*. New York, 1972.

Vance, Vick, and Pierre Lauer. *Hussein King of Jordan: My "War" with Israel*. London, 1969.

Wasserstein, Bernard. *The British in Palestine: The Mandatory Government and the Arab-Jewish Conflict 1917–1929*. London, 1978.

Weizmann, Chaim. *The Letters and Papers of Chaim Weizmann*. Jerusalem, 1977. Vols. VIII–X.

———. *Trial and Error*. New York, 1949.

Whiteman, Marjorie M. *Digest of International Law*. Vol. 2. Washington, 1963.

Wilson, Harold. *The Chariot of Israel*. New York, 1981.

Woodward, E. L. and R. Butler, eds. *Documents on British Foreign Policy, 1919–1939*. 1st Series. Vol. IV. London, 1952.

Zangwill, Israel. "Nordau." *Jewish Standard*, January 25, 1984.

Ziff, William B. *The Rape of Palestine*. New York, 1938.

Index

Abdul-Hamid II, 2–3, 28
Abdullah ibn Hussein, 4, 8–10, 12–13, 69, 79–109, 126, 140, 148, 153; annexes West Bank, 108; assassinated, 109; declared king of Iraq, 69–70; derives lessons from Arab-Israel war, 100–101; enters Transjordan, 80–81; meets with Golda Meir, 94, 97; meets with Weizmann, 86; recognized as Emir by Britain, 87; secret negotiations with Israel, 106; seeks British intervention in Hejaz, 7
Abu-Awda, Adnan, 142
Abu-Khalid, Muhammad, 89
Abul Huda, Tawfiq Pasha, 95, 107
Ahmad, king of Yemen, 112
al-Ajam, Salim Pasha Abu, 89
Aldington, Richard, 23
Ali ibn Hussein, 79
Ali, Muhammad Kurd, 25
Allenby, General, 23–25, 54, 65, 70, 75
Allied Supreme Council, 60–62, 71

American Commission of Inquiry (King-Crane), 66
Anglo-French: agreement of September 1919, 67; relations, 17
Anglo-Transjordanian Treaty, 100
Antonius, George, 59
Arab: nationalists, 4, 12, 32, 48, 92; revolt against Turkey, 21
Arab Bureau in Cairo, 17, 25, 49, 54
Arab Defense Pact of 1964, 120
Arab Government of All Palestine, 103–4, 107
Arab Higher Committee, 91–92
Arab League, 94, 96, 100, 103–5, 107–9, 113–14, 116, 118, 139; designates PLO as sole representative of Palestinians, 139
Arab Legion, 93, 95–97, 99
Arab Palestine National Assembly, 103
Arab Summit Conference (Rabat), 141
Arafat, Yasser, 129–130, 132, 135, 137–38, 141–45; becomes chair-

171

Index

man of PLO, 133; claims Jordan as Palestinian territory, 141
Assad, Hafez, 137
Auda Abu Tayeh, 22–23
Avineri, Shlomo, 135

Baha ad-Din, Ahmad, 127
Baha ad-Din Bey, 29–30
Balfour Declaration, 25, 44–48, 50, 58, 60, 71, 84, 86
Balfour, Lord Arthur, 41, 44–45, 49, 67, 76, 84, 86
Barbour, Walwaorth, 125
Begin, Menahem, 147–148; autonomy plan for West Bank, 148–49
Ben-Gurion, David, 30, 87, 97–98, 107
Ben-Zvi, Yitzhak, 30
Bernadotte, Count Folke, 99
Bevin, Ernest, 95
Bryce, Lord, 54
Bull, Odd, 122
Bussche-Haddenhausen, Freiherr Axel von dem, 47

Cairo conference, 81, 86
Camp, Major, 78
Camp David agreements, 141–42, 148, 155
Carter, Jimmy, 142, 151
Cecil, Lord Robert, 42
Chamberlain, Austen, 16
Churchill, Sir Winston, 81–83, 86; makes Abdullah ruler, 82–83
Clayton, Gilbert, 15, 48–50, 53, 55; denial of British intent with regard to Hussein, 17
Clemenceau, George, 51, 69, 76
Cohen, B. W., 68
Comité Central Syrien of Paris: declaration to Peace Conference, 61

Committee of Union and Progress, 2, 4, 18, 37
Cornwallis, Kinnahan: disputes Clayton, 49
Crewe, Lord: message to Allied governments, 35
Crowe, Sir Eyre, 55
Curzon, Lord, 38, 46, 66–67, 69, 73–74, 76–78

Damascus: fall of, 25–26; protocol, 12–14
Danin, Ezra, 94, 97
Daoud, Muhammad, 136
Dayan, Moshe, 106–107, 123, 140–41
Declaration to the Seven, 65
Djemal Pasha, 18–19, 24, 29, 31

Eder, David, 55; meets with Feisal, 73
Eshkol, Levi, 121–22, 125–26; urges Hussein not to enter war, 122, 140
Eytan, Walter, 106

al-Faiz, Mithqal Pasha, 89
Farouk, King, 104–5
al-Faruqi, Muhammad, 16
al-Faruqi, Suleiman Taji, 105
Fatah, 116–119, 130, 132, 138; reversal of Nasser's strategy, 116
Fedayeen, 110–11, 116–17, 128–38; abandoned by Assad, 137; take over PLO, 132; threat to stability of Jordan, 131
Feisal ibn Hussein, 10, 18–20, 22–26, 52–77, 79–80, 82–83, 87, 90; agreement with Weizmann, 57–59, 66, 68, 70; appointed king of Iraq, 74; confrontation with Djemal Pasha, 18–19; letter to

Index

Frankfurter, 63–64, 68; elected king of Syria, 69; expelled from Syria, 72; meets with Weizmann, 52, 55, 67; mission to Damascus, 12–13; seeks Zionist financial support, 54–55; signs and repudiates agreement with French, 69
Feisal II, 111–12
France: demands Britain pacify Transjordan, 78; geopolitical goals, 32; mandate over Syria, 71; ultimatum to Feisal, 72
Frankfurter, Felix, 62–63
Front of National Sacrifice: Hussein's fedayeen organization, 131

Ganem, Chekri, 61
Germany: declaration of support for Zionists, 47; foreign ministry documents, 10; war plans, 6
Glubb, John Bagot, 95–97, 99
Goldie, Desmond, 96–97
Graham, Sir Ronald, 43–47
Great Britain, 5, 11–12, 14; appoints Feisal as king of Iraq, 74; concern about Turco-German alliance, 5–6; grants Transjordan independence, 93; mandate over Mesopotamia and Palestine, 71, 74; perceptions of Jewish influence in Turkey, 36–37; recognizes Abdullah, 87; royal commission proposes partition, 91; ruler of largest Muslim population, 6; strategic interests, 36; war planning, 9. *See also* Palestine Mandate
Grey, Sir Edward, 13, 33, 35

al-Hadi, Abd, 61
Haganah, 97
Hall, William R., 33
Harkabi, Yehoshafat, 149
Hashemites: claims to Hejaz, 18; hegemony over tribes, 3; position in Arabia, 1–2
Hejaz: strategic significance, 6–7
Hejaz Railway, 2–5, 32, 34, 75, 81, 84; religious and strategic significance, 5, 60, 75
Herzl, Theodor, 27–28, 30; proposal to sultan, 27
Hilmi Pasha, Ahmad, 103
Hirtzel, Sir Arthur: India Office memorandum, 15
Hogarth, D. G.: blocks Weizmann-Hussein meeting, 54
Holy places of Islam, 1–2, 10
Holy war, 9; declared by Ottomans, 11
Hussein ibn Talal, 109–10, 112–31, 133–45, 148, 151, 153, 155; federation plan, 138, 141–43, 152; meets with Dayan, 141; moves against PLO, 135–38; rejects Camp David accords, 141–142; snubbed by Nasser, 121; supports Fatah against Nasser, 116; taunts Nasser, 119; withdraws recognition of PLO, 118–19
Hussein ibn Ali, 1–11, 15–25, 32, 37, 48, 54, 74, 79, 90; expected to cooperate in Turkish attack on Suez Canal, 6; offers allegiance to Britain, 13; receives payments from Germans and British, 11; seeks position of sherif of Mecca, 2–3; threatens insurrection, 4
al-Husseini, Haj Amin, 89, 91, 94, 103
Hussein-McMahon correspondence, 13–18, 35, 47, 73

Ibn Saud, Abdul Aziz, 91

173

Index

al-Ilah, Abd, 111
India, Government of, 15
India Office, 10, 15, 19
Inter-Allied Conference (St. Jean de Maurienne), 38–39

al-Jabari, Muhammad Ali, 105
Jabotinsky, Vladimir, 31, 48
Jarring, Gunnar, 125
Jewish Agency for Palestine, 89, 93–94
Jewish Legion, 31, 48
Johnson, Lyndon, 125
Jordan Option, 147, 151–53, 155
Joyce, Pierre C.: memorandum on Weizmann-Feisal meeting, 53

Kamal, Mohamed, 152
Kemal, Mustafa (Ataturk), 70
Khammash, Amer, 120
al-Khaza'i, Rashid Pasha, 89
Kilani, Rasoul, 133
Kirkbride, Alec, 78–81, 85, 98, 106
Kirkbride, Alan, 78
Kissinger, Henry, 136–37; asks Israel to intervene on behalf of Jordan, 136
Kitchener, Lord General, 8, 11, 13; implicitly offers caliphate to Hussein, 9; meets with Abdullah, 7Lansing, Robert, 62

Lawrence, T. E., 21, 23, 25, 52, 59, 63, 83–85; warning to Hussein, 24
League of Nations, 85–87, 92
Lebanon: declares independence of Syria, 70
Lichtheim, Richard, 31
Lloyd George, David, 37, 51, 84; understanding of Balfour Declaration, 46

McMahon, Sir Henry, 20, 32, 37
Maysalun, Day of, 72
Meinertzhagen, Richard, 63, 85
Meir (Myerson), Golda, 94, 97; meets with Abdullah, 94, 97
Milner, Lord, 25
Moab, National Government of, 78, 81
Moltke, Count von: letter to foreign ministry, 6
Montagu, Sir Edwin, 44–45, 57
al-Mulqi, Fawzi, 95

Naor, Arye, 148
al-Nashashibi, Nasir ad-Din, 98
Nasser, Gamal Abdel, 111–16, 118–22, 128, 137, 140; orders blockade of Straits of Tiran, 120
Nasser bin Gamil, Sherif, 131
Nevlinski, P. M., 28
Nicolson, Harold, 41
Nixon, Richard M., 137
Nordau, Max: first formulation of Zionist aim, 28

O'Beirne, Hugh, 37
Occupied Enemy Territory Administration (OETA), 54
Ormsby-Gore, W., 50, 92
Ottoman Empire: promotion of pan-Islam, 6; dismantling of, 32

Palestine Liberation Army (PLA), 115, 136
Palestine Liberation Organization (PLO), 113–19, 121, 126–27, 132–134, 137–145, 150, 155; relocates to Lebanon, 138
Palestine Mandate, 77, 81, 83, 85–86, 93–94
Palestine National Council (PNC), 114, 127, 132–133, 137–38, 140

Index

Palestinian National Covenant, 115, 127, 132
Patterson, John H., 48
Peace Conference (Paris), 56–57, 61–62, 64, 79
Peled, Mattityahu, 129, 153
Picot, Georges, 22, 33, 40
Popular Front for the Liberation of Palestine, 135

Qadri, Ahmad, 61

Rabin, Yitzhak, 136–37
Rafael, Giseon, 125
Reagan, Ronald, 143
Reagan Plan, 143–44
Riad, Abdel Moneim, 122
Rida, Muhammad Rashid, 22
ar-Rifai, Samir Pasha, 107
Rifai, Zaid, 136
Rogers Plan, 134, 143
Rothschild, Lord James, 46
Russia: expansionism, 5; interest in holy places, 34
Russian Revolution: implications of, 48

Sacher, Harry, 68
Sadat, Anwar, 139, 141
as-Said, Nuri, 112
Said Pasha, 68
Sami, Shams-ud-Din Bey, 89–90
Samuel, Sir Herbert, 41, 45, 54, 68, 73, 76–81, 83, 87–88
San Remo Conference, 50, 71–72, 74, 77
Sasson, Eliahu, 94
Sazanov, S. D., 36, 39
Shamir, Yitzhak, 147
Shamir, Shlomo, 97
Sharaf, Abd al-Hamid, 142
Sharon, Ariel, 142, 151

Sherif of Mecca, 1–6, 9, 16, 20
Shertok (Sharett), Moshe, 93
Shihadeh, Aziz, 129
Shiloah, Reuven, 106
Shuqairy, Ahmad, 114–15, 117–18, 121
Sieff, Israel: argument for retention of Trans-Jordan, 34
Smuts, Jan, 38
Sokolow, Nahum, 44
Somerset, Major, 78
Storrs, Ronald, 7–9, 13
Sublime Porte, 2, 3, 8, 10, 18–19
Suez Canal: in war plans, 5–6
Sweidani, Ahmad, 116
Sykes, Sir Mark, 22, 33–34, 39–41; scheme to use Zionists, 39–40
Sykes-Picot agreement, 16, 25, 33–37, 39, 42–43, 47, 51, 54–55, 60, 71, 84
Syria: strategic importance, 32
Syrian General (National) Congress, 69, 71

al-Tal, Wasfi, 123
Talal ibn Abdullah, 109
al-Talhouni, Bahajat, 129
Toynbee, Arnold, 17
Transjordan-Israel Armistice Agreement, 100
Trumpeldor, Joseph, 32, 70
Turkey, 4; enters war, 9; plans to replace Hussein, 12; proposed dual monarchy with Syria, 71

Umm Qeis Treaty, 78
United Nations, 94–95, 98–100, 104–5, 110, 125, 148
U Thant, 119–20

Village Leagues, 142–43

175

Index

Weizmann, Chaim, 33–34, 42–43, 48–49, 52–59, 63, 65, 67–68, 70, 76, 81, 85–87, 89–90; agreement with Feisal, 57–59, 66, 68, 70; defines "Jewish national home," 62; meets with Abdullah, 86; meets with Feisal, 52, 55–58, 67
Wingate, Sir Reginald, 15
Wilson, Brigadier, 26

Yale, William, 56

Young Turks, 2, 4, 7, 37
Zeid bin Shaker, 120
Zeid ibn Hussein, 24
Zionist: congresses, 28, 29, 85, 88; territorial claims, 42–43, 60, 71, 76, 81; yishuv (settlement), 30
Zionist Commission, 48–49, 56, 66, 73
Zionist Organization, 29–30, 42, 48, 91
Zion Mule Corps, 32, 48
Zurikat, Mitri Pasha, 89